I0009083

ADVANCED DUNGEONS & DYNAMICS 365 IMPLEMENTATION GUIDE

THE WATERDEEP TRADING COMPANY PROJECT

MODULE 4: CONFIGURING WAREHOUSES AND PRODUCTS

MURRAY FIFE

© 2019 Blind Squirrel Publishing, LLC, All Rights Reserved

All Rights Reserved

ISBN-13: 978-1077209299

www.dynamicscompanions.com
Dynamics Companions

- 2 -

www.blindsquirrelpublishing.com
© 2019 Blind Squirrel Publishing, LLC , All Rights Reserved

BLIND SQUIRREL
PUBLISHING

Preface

I have been reviving an old project that started a while ago and have started up a new project blog to track the progress. Being a lifelong fan of Dungeons & Dragons, with the unfortunate problem that I cannot find anyone to play with I have decided to create a test implementation Dynamics 365 in the AD&D format just to see how it would work and if I can find some creative ways to use Dynamics 365 and chose to implement the **Waterdeep Trading Company** as an example where I can track their many legal (and not so legal) entities within Faerûn.

www.dynamicscompanions.com
Dynamics Companions

- 3 -

www.blindsquirrelpublishing.com
© 2019 Blind Squirrel Publishing, LLC , All Rights Reserved

BLIND SQUIRREL
PUBLISHING

www.blindsquirrelpublishing.com
© 2019 Blind Squirrel Publishing, LLC , All Rights Reserved

BLIND SQUIRREL
PUBLISHING

Table of Contents

dync
dynamics companions
www.dynamicscompanions.com
Dynamics Companions

- 5 -

www.blindsquirrelpublishing.com
© 2019 Blind Squirrel Publishing, LLC , All Rights Reserved

BLIND SQUIRREL
PUBLISHING

www.blindsquirrelpublishing.com
© 2019 Blind Squirrel Publishing, LLC, All Rights Reserved

BLIND SQUIRREL
PUBLISHING

Introduction

The **Waterdeep Trading Company** is the purveyor of all the finest adventuring supplies to travelers, rogues, wizards and clerics in all Faerûn. That means that we will need to track all the finest adventuring supplies.

In this module, we will walk through the setup of the **Waterdeep Trading Company** store and warehouse with its different locations, and then start registering the products that we will be purchasing, inventorying and selling.

Configuring the Warehouse and Locations

The **Waterdeep Trading Company** is just a small store right now and is organized in different areas for adventuring gear, armory, and weapons, stables, an apothecary, and we even have a library full of the finest tomes in the realms.

To track all the inventory that we have, we will want to model the store locations as a warehouse within Dynamics 365 so that we know exactly where the inventory is, and so that we can easily find the products when we are looking for them.

Topics Covered

- Creating a Store Site
- Creating a Store Warehouse
- Creating Aisles Locations within the Store Warehouse
- Creating Locations within the Store Warehouse

Creating a Store Site

All the warehouses that we will need to set up for the **Waterdeep Trading Company** will be grouped into groups called **Sites.** As the company grows, then we may have more than one location within the same site, like a distribution warehouse, a production area and more.

So to start, we will create a main site for the **Waterdeep** area which we can start to add our warehouses to.

Topics Covered

- Opening the Site maintenance form

- Adding a new Site

Opening the Site maintenance form

To create our **Site** we will need to open the **Site** maintenance form.

How to do it...

Step 1: Open the Sites form through the menu search

We can find the **Sites** form is through the menu search feature.

Type in **sties** into the menu search and select **Sites**.

Opening the Site maintenance form

How to do it...

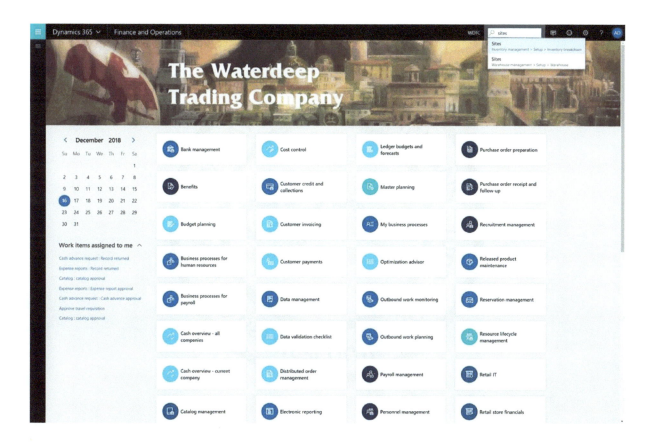

Step 1: Open the Sites form through the menu search

We can find the **Sites** form is through the menu search feature.

We can do this by clicking on the search icon in the header of the form (or by pressing **ALT+G**) and then type in **sties** into the search box. Then you will be able to select the **Sites** form from the dropdown list.

dync
dynamics companions

www.dynamicscompanions.com
Dynamics Companions

- 11 -

www.blindsquirrelpublishing.com
© 2019 Blind Squirrel Publishing, LLC , All Rights Reserved

BLIND SQUIRREL
PUBLISHING

Opening the Site maintenance form

How to do it...

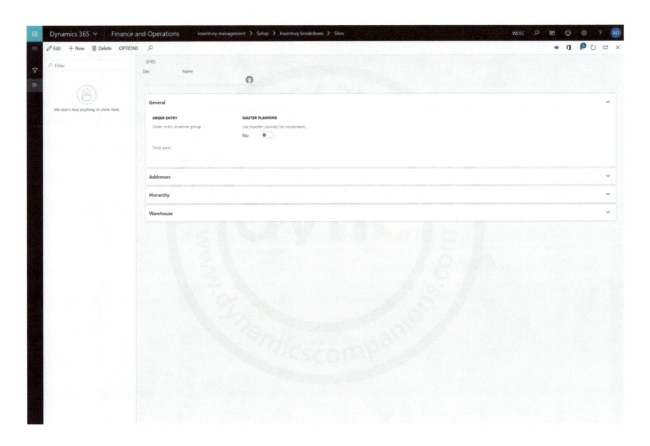

Step 1: Open the Sites form through the menu search

This will open the Sites maintenance form where we will be able to add all the sites that we will link our warehouses to.

dync
www.dynamicscompanions.com
Dynamics Companions

- 12 -

www.blindsquirrelpublishing.com
© 2019 Blind Squirrel Publishing, LLC , All Rights Reserved

BLIND SQUIRREL
PUBLISHING

Adding a new Site

Now we will want to add our first site, which will be for the **Waterdeep** location.

How to do it...

Step 1: Click on the New button

To do this, we will create a new Site record.

Click on the **New** button.

Step 2: Update the Site

We will now want to give our Site a reference code to identify the site.

Set the **Site** to **WD**.

Step 3: Update the Name

And then we will give our Site a more descriptive name that will help people decipher the site code.

Set the **Name** to **Waterdeep**.

Step 4: Click on the Save button

After we have done that, we can save the record, and we are done with the site setup.

Click on the **Save** button.

dync
www.dynamicscompanions.com
Dynamics Companions

- 13 -

www.blindsquirrelpublishing.com
© 2019 Blind Squirrel Publishing, LLC , All Rights Reserved
 BLIND SQUIRREL PUBLISHING

Adding a new Site

How to do it...

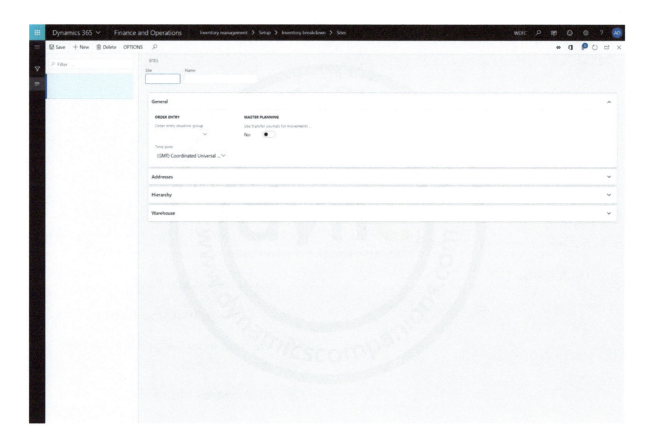

Step 1: Click on the New button

To do this, we will create a new Site record.

To do this just click on the **New** button.

dync
dynamics companions

www.dynamicscompanions.com
Dynamics Companions

- 14 -

www.blindsquirrelpublishing.com
© 2019 Blind Squirrel Publishing, LLC , All Rights Reserved

BLIND SQUIRREL
PUBLISHING

Adding a new Site

How to do it...

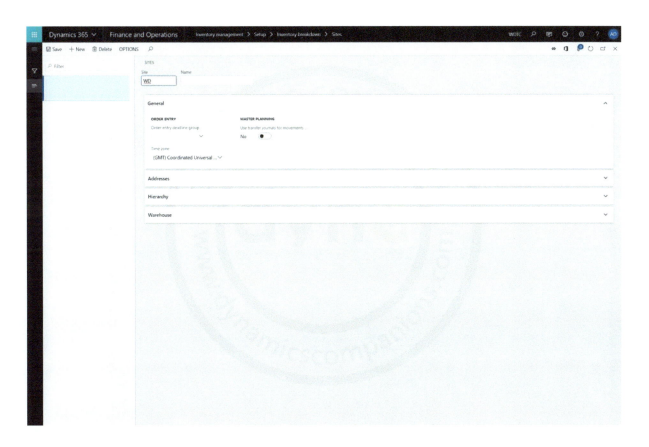

Step 2: Update the Site

We will now want to give our Site a reference code to identify the site.

To do this update the **Site** value.

For this example, we will want to set the **Site** to **WD**.

dync
www.dynamicscompanions.com
Dynamics Companions

- 15 -

www.blindsquirrelpublishing.com
© 2019 Blind Squirrel Publishing, LLC , All Rights Reserved

BLIND SQUIRREL
PUBLISHING

Adding a new Site

How to do it...

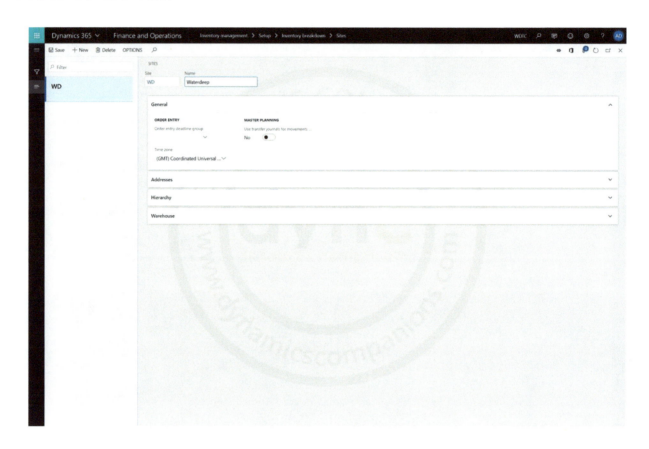

Step 3: Update the Name

And then we will give our Site a more descriptive name that will help people decipher the site code.

To do this change the **Name** value.

This time, we will want to set the **Name** to **Waterdeep**.

dync
www.dynamicscompanions.com
Dynamics Companions

- 16 -

www.blindsquirrelpublishing.com
© 2019 Blind Squirrel Publishing, LLC , All Rights Reserved

BLIND SQUIRREL
PUBLISHING

Adding a new Site

How to do it...

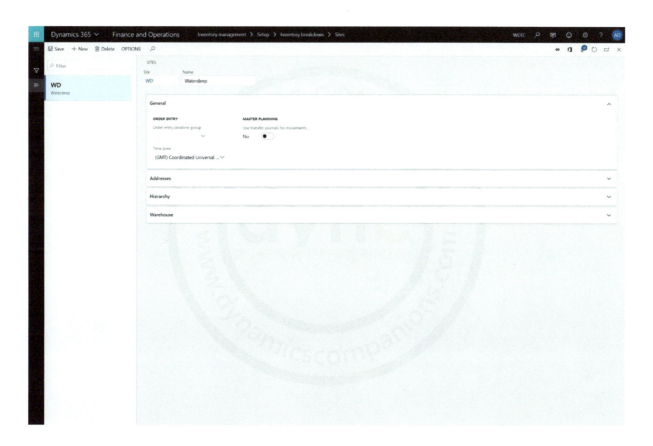

Step 4: Click on the Save button

After we have done that, we can save the record, and we are done with the site setup.

To do this, all we need to do is click on the **Save** button.

dyn c
dynamics companions

www.dynamicscompanions.com
Dynamics Companions

- 17 -

www.blindsquirrelpublishing.com
© 2019 Blind Squirrel Publishing, LLC , All Rights Reserved

BLIND SQUIRREL
PUBLISHING

Review

How easy was that? Now we have a site that we can attach

www.dynamicscompanions.com
Dynamics Companions

- 18 -

www.blindsquirrelpublishing.com
© 2019 Blind Squirrel Publishing, LLC , All Rights Reserved

BLIND SQUIRREL
PUBLISHING

Creating a Store Warehouse

Now that we have created our site, we can set up our Warehouses, and we will start by creating one to manage all of the inventory and stock that we have in the main store for the **Waterdeep Trading Company**.

Topics Covered

- Opening the Warehouse maintenance form

- Creating a new Warehouse

dync
dynamics companions
www.dynamicscompanions.com
Dynamics Companions

- 19 -

www.blindsquirrelpublishing.com
© 2019 Blind Squirrel Publishing, LLC , All Rights Reserved

BLIND SQUIRREL
PUBLISHING

Opening the Warehouse maintenance form

To do this we will need to find the maintenance form for the warehouses.

How to do it...

Step 1: Open the Warehouses form through the menu search

We can find the **Warehouses** form is through the menu search feature.

Type in **warehouses** into the menu search and select **Warehouses**.

Opening the Warehouse maintenance form

How to do it...

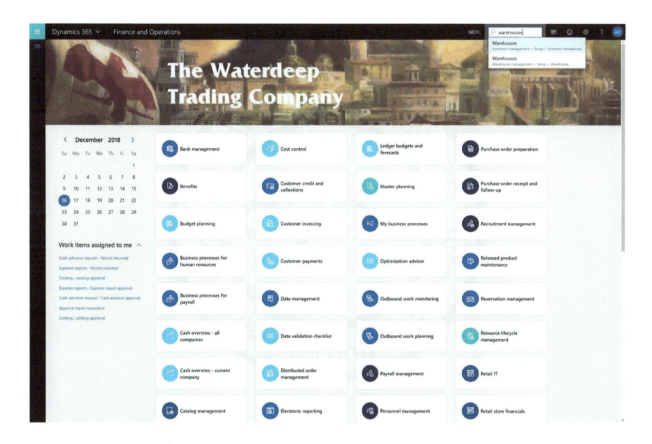

Step 1: Open the Warehouses form through the menu search

We can find the **Warehouses** form is through the menu search feature.

We can do this by clicking on the search icon in the header of the form (or by pressing **ALT+G**) and then type in **warehouses** into the search box. Then you will be able to select the **Warehouses** form from the dropdown list.

dync
dynamics companions

www.dynamicscompanions.com
Dynamics Companions

- 21 -

www.blindsquirrelpublishing.com
© 2019 Blind Squirrel Publishing, LLC, All Rights Reserved

BLIND SQUIRREL
PUBLISHING

Opening the Warehouse maintenance form

How to do it...

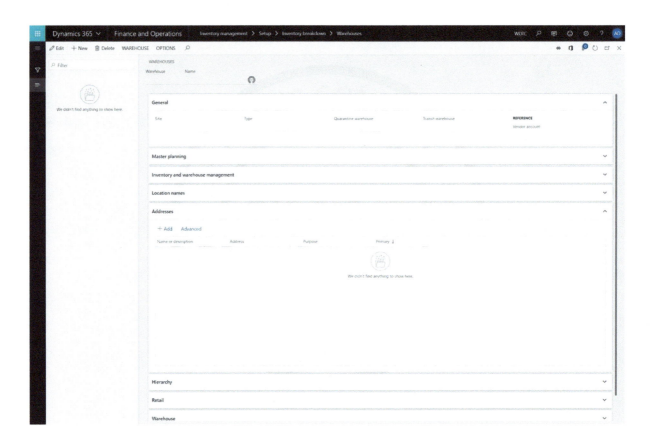

Step 1: Open the Warehouses form through the menu search

This opens up the Warehouse maintenance form where we will be able to add as many warehouses as we like to the system.

dync
dynamics companions

www.dynamicscompanions.com
Dynamics Companions

- 22 -

www.blindsquirrelpublishing.com
© 2019 Blind Squirrel Publishing, LLC , All Rights Reserved

BLIND SQUIRREL
PUBLISHING

Creating a new Warehouse

Now we will want to create our first warehouse for the **Waterdeep Trading Company** store.

How to do it...

Step 1: Click on the New button

To do this, we will want to create a new **Warehouse** record.

Click on the **New** button.

Step 2: Update the Warehouse

Next, we will want to add an identification code for the Warehouse as a shorthand to reference it by.

Set the Warehouse to WDSTORE.

Step 3: Update the Name

And then we will want to add a more descriptive name for the warehouse.

Set the Name to Waterdeep Store.

Step 4: Select the Site

Then we will want to associate the warehouse with the Site that we just created.

Click on the **Site** dropdown list And choose **WD**.

Step 5: Expand Location names tab

Next, we will want to specify the types of locations that we will track within the warehouse, and we do this by tweaking the **Location names** flags in the warehouse.

Expand the **Location names** tab.

Step 6: Change the Include aisle

Our warehouse locations won't be too elaborate, we are just going to break down the locations by area, and we will use Aisles to separate the inventory.

Change the **Include aisle** switch And set it to **Yes**.

Step 7: Click on the Save button

After we have done that we are done with the setup of the warehouse, and we can save the record and then exit from the form.

Click on the **Save** button.

www.dynamicscompanions.com
Dynamics Companions

- 23 -

www.blindsquirrelpublishing.com
© 2019 Blind Squirrel Publishing, LLC , All Rights Reserved

BLIND SQUIRREL
PUBLISHING

Creating a new Warehouse

How to do it...

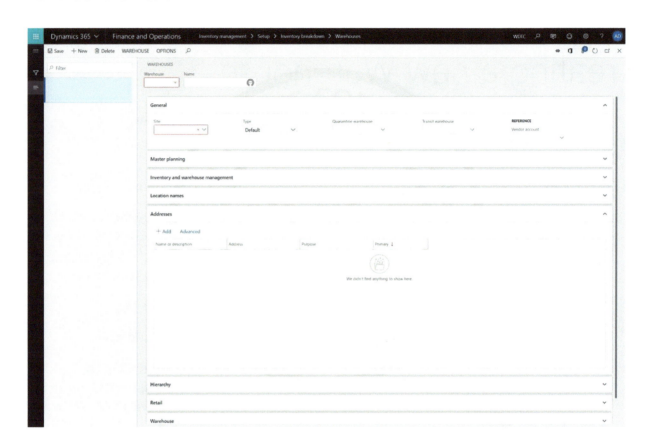

Step 1: Click on the New button

To do this, we will want to create a new **Warehouse** record.

To do this, all we need to do is click on the **New** button.

dync
dynamics companions
www.dynamicscompanions.com
Dynamics Companions

- 24 -

www.blindsquirrelpublishing.com
© 2019 Blind Squirrel Publishing, LLC , All Rights Reserved

BLIND SQUIRREL
PUBLISHING

Creating a new Warehouse

How to do it...

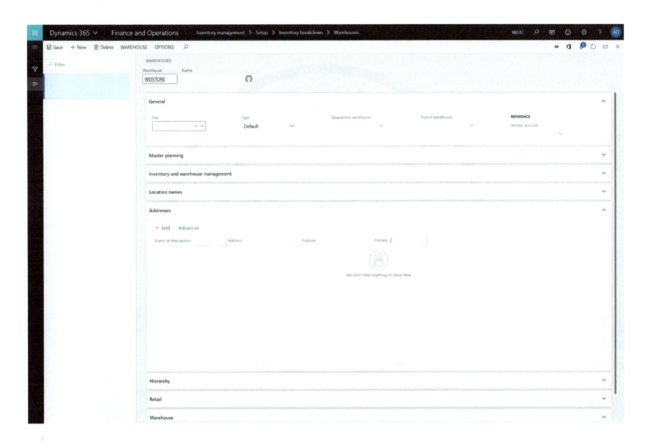

Step 2: Update the Warehouse

Next, we will want to add an identification code for the Warehouse as a shorthand to reference it by.

To do this just change the **Warehouse** value.

For this example, we will want to set the **Warehouse** to **WDSTORE**.

www.dynamicscompanions.com
Dynamics Companions

- 25 -

www.blindsquirrelpublishing.com
© 2019 Blind Squirrel Publishing, LLC , All Rights Reserved

BLIND SQUIRREL
PUBLISHING

Creating a new Warehouse

How to do it...

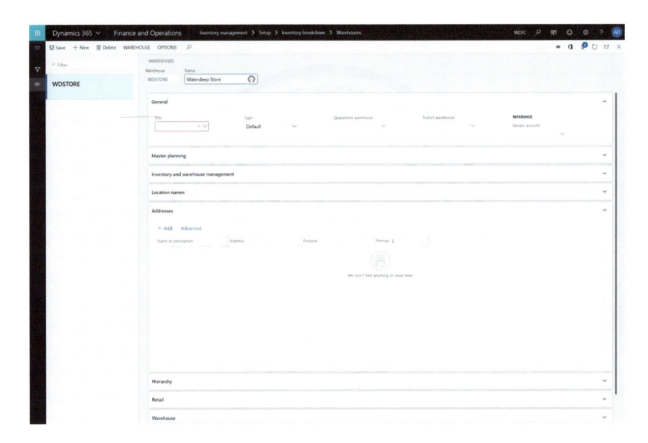

Step 3: Update the Name

And then we will want to add a more descriptive name for the warehouse.

To do this just change the **Name** value.

For this example, we will want to set the **Name** to **Waterdeep Store**.

dync
www.dynamicscompanions.com
Dynamics Companions

- 26 -

www.blindsquirrelpublishing.com
© 2019 Blind Squirrel Publishing, LLC , All Rights Reserved

BLIND SQUIRREL
PUBLISHING

Creating a new Warehouse

How to do it...

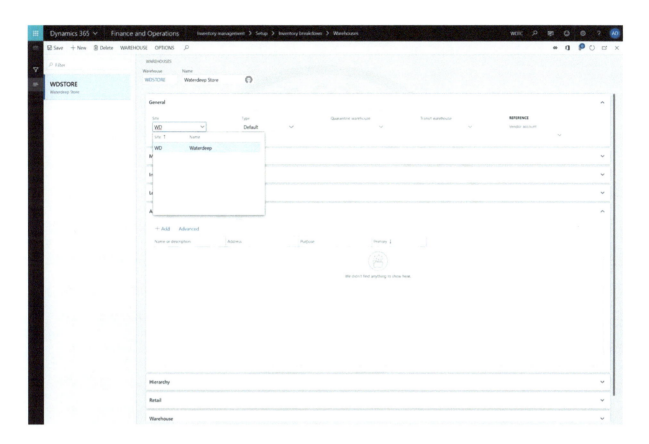

Step 4: Select the Site

Then we will want to associate the warehouse with the Site that we just created.

To do this just select the **Site** value from the dropdown list.

For this example, we will want to click on the **Site** dropdown list and pick **WD**.

dync
www.dynamicscompanions.com
Dynamics Companions

- 27 -

www.blindsquirrelpublishing.com
© 2019 Blind Squirrel Publishing, LLC , All Rights Reserved

BLIND SQUIRREL
PUBLISHING

Creating a new Warehouse

How to do it...

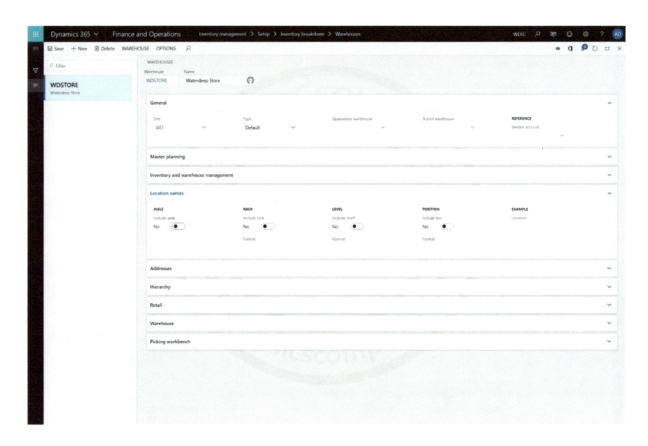

Step 5: Expand Location names tab

Next, we will want to specify the types of locations that we will track within the warehouse, and we do this by tweaking the **Location names** flags in the warehouse.

To do this, all we need to do is expand the **Location names** tab.

www.dynamicscompanions.com
Dynamics Companions

- 28 -

www.blindsquirrelpublishing.com
© 2019 Blind Squirrel Publishing, LLC, All Rights Reserved

BLIND SQUIRREL
PUBLISHING

Creating a new Warehouse

How to do it...

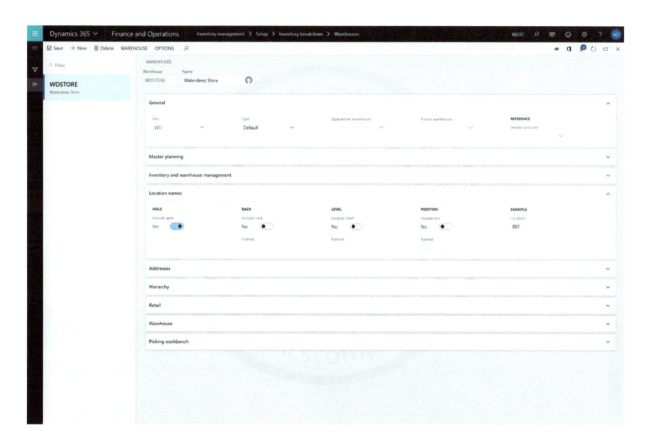

Step 6: Change the Include aisle

Our warehouse locations won't be too elaborate, we are just going to break down the locations by area, and we will use Aisles to separate the inventory.

To do this, we will just need to change the **Include aisle** value.

This time, we will want to click on the **Include aisle** toggle switch and change it to the **Yes** value.

dync
dynamics companions
www.dynamicscompanions.com
Dynamics Companions
- 29 -
www.blindsquirrelpublishing.com
© 2019 Blind Squirrel Publishing, LLC , All Rights Reserved
BLIND SQUIRREL
PUBLISHING

Creating a new Warehouse

How to do it...

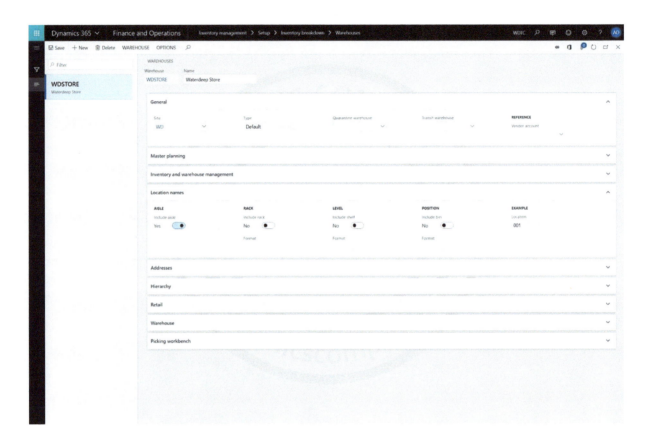

Step 7: Click on the Save button

After we have done that we are done with the setup of the warehouse, and we can save the record and then exit from the form.

To do this just click on the **Save** button.

dynamicscompanions.com
Dynamics Companions

- 30 -

www.blindsquirrelpublishing.com
© 2019 Blind Squirrel Publishing, LLC , All Rights Reserved

BLIND SQUIRREL
PUBLISHING

Review

How easy was that. In just a couple of minutes, we set up a new Warehouse in the system that is linked to the **Waterdeep** site.

Creating Aisles Locations within the Store Warehouse

Now that we have our warehouse configured we will want to set up the different aisle types that we will have within the warehouse. In the next step, we will use these to create the inventory locations within the **Waterdeep Trading Company Store**.

Topics Covered

- Opening the Aisle maintenance form

- Creating new Aisle locations

Opening the Aisle maintenance form

To do this we will want to find the **Aisle** maintenance form.

How to do it...

Step 1: Open the Inventory aisles form through the menu search

We can find the **Inventory aisles** form is through the menu search feature.

Type in **inventory ai** into the menu search and select **Inventory aisles**.

dync
dynamics companions

www.dynamicscompanions.com
Dynamics Companions

- 33 -

www.blindsquirrelpublishing.com
© 2019 Blind Squirrel Publishing, LLC , All Rights Reserved

BLIND SQUIRREL
PUBLISHING

Opening the Aisle maintenance form

How to do it...

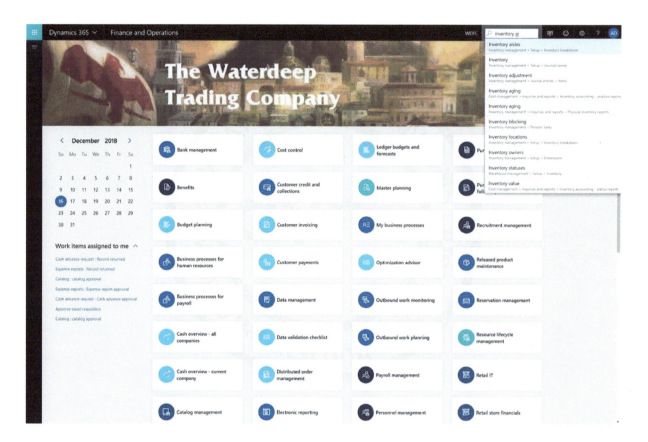

Step 1: Open the Inventory aisles form through the menu search

We can find the **Inventory aisles** form is through the menu search feature.

We can do this by clicking on the search icon in the header of the form (or by pressing **ALT+G**) and then type in **inventory ai** into the search box. Then you will be able to select the **Inventory aisles** form from the dropdown list.

dync
dynamics companions

www.dynamicscompanions.com
Dynamics Companions

- 34 -

www.blindsquirrelpublishing.com
© 2019 Blind Squirrel Publishing, LLC, All Rights Reserved

BLIND SQUIRREL
PUBLISHING

Opening the Aisle maintenance form

How to do it...

Step 1: Open the Inventory aisles form through the menu search

This will open up the **Aisle** maintenance form where we will be able to set up all of the different Aisle location types.

dync
dynamics companions

www.dynamicscompanions.com
Dynamics Companions

- 35 -

www.blindsquirrelpublishing.com
© 2019 Blind Squirrel Publishing, LLC , All Rights Reserved

BLIND SQUIRREL
PUBLISHING

Creating new Aisle locations

Now we will want to set up some different types of Aisles that we will use within our warehouse.

How to do it...

Step 1: Click on the New button

Let's start by setting up our first Aisle location.

Click on the **New** button.

Step 2: Select the Warehouse

We will then want to select the Warehouse that we want to associate our new Aisle location to.

Click on the **Warehouse** dropdown list And select **WDSTORE**.

Step 3: Update the Aisle

Now we will be able to name our Aisle.

Set the **Aisle** to **GEAR**.

Step 4: Update the Name

And to finish off, we will want to give our aisle a more descriptive name.

Set the Name to Gear Aisle.

Step 5: Click on the New button

Let's continue on and set up some of the other aisles that we will manage within the warehouse.

Click on the **New** button.

Step 6: Select the Warehouse

We will want to select our warehouse that the aisle will be associated with.

Click on the **Warehouse** dropdown list And select **WDSTORE**.

Step 7: Update the Aisle

We can now give our aisle a code that we will use to reference it.

Set the **Aisle** to **ARMORY**.

Step 8: Update the Name

And finally, we will give our aisle a more descriptive name.

Set the Name to Armory Aisle.

Step 9: Click on the New button

Let's add another aisle, for all of the books that we will be selling at the Waterdeep Trading Company store.

Click on the **New** button.

Step 10: Choose the Warehouse

We will want to select our warehouse again that we will be associating the aisle with.

Click on the **Warehouse** dropdown list And select **WDSTORE**.

 www.dynamicscompanions.com
Dynamics Companions

- 36 -

www.blindsquirrelpublishing.com
© 2019 Blind Squirrel Publishing, LLC , All Rights Reserved

BLIND SQUIRREL
PUBLISHING

Step 11: Update the Aisle

Now we will assign our aisle a code to reference it by.

Set the **Aisle** to **LIBRARY**.

Step 12: Update the Name

And then we will add a more descriptive name to the aisle.

Set the **Name** to **Library**.

Step 13: Click on the New button

We will add a couple more aisle locations, and the next Aisle will be where we will store all of our ingredients and medications.

Click on the **New** button.

Step 14: Select the Warehouse

We will select our warehouse for the aisle.

Click on the **Warehouse** dropdown list And select **WDSTORE**.

Step 15: Update the Aisle

We will give our aisle a code to reference it by.

Set the Aisle to APOTHECARY.

Step 16: Update the Name

And then we will give our apothecary aisle a more descriptive name.

Set the Name to Apothecary.

Step 17: Click on the New button

Let's add one last aisle to the warehouse, for the stables.

Click on the **New** button.

Step 18: Choose the Warehouse

Let's link this aisle to our warehouse.

Click on the **Warehouse** dropdown list And select **WDSTORE**.

Step 19: Update the Aisle

We will then give our Stable aisle a code that we can identify it by.

Set the **Aisle** to **STABLE**.

Step 20: Update the Name

And finally, we will give our aisle a proper name to accompany the code.

Set the **Name** to **Stable**.

Creating new Aisle locations

How to do it...

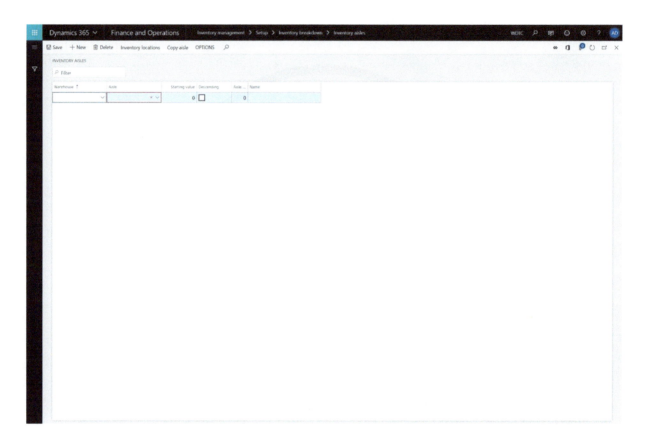

Step 1: Click on the New button

Let's start by setting up our first Aisle location.

To do this, all we need to do is click on the **New** button.

dync
dynamics companions

BLIND SQUIRREL
PUBLISHING

Creating new Aisle locations

How to do it...

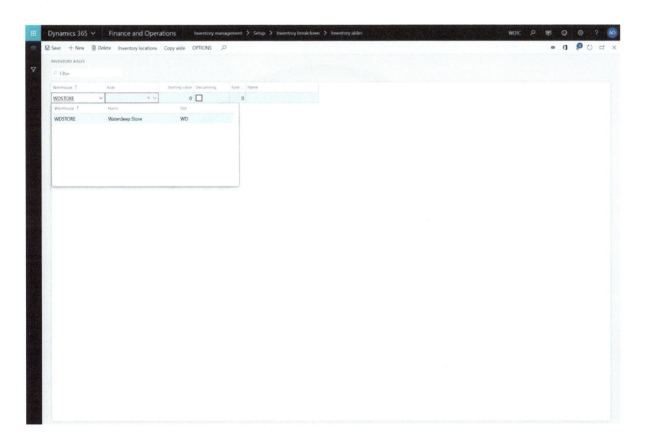

Step 2: Select the Warehouse

We will then want to select the Warehouse that we want to associate our new Aisle location to.

To do this just pick the **Warehouse** option from the dropdown list.

For this example, we will want to click on the **Warehouse** dropdown list and pick **WDSTORE**.

www.dynamicscompanions.com
Dynamics Companions

- 39 -

www.blindsquirrelpublishing.com
© 2019 Blind Squirrel Publishing, LLC , All Rights Reserved

BLIND SQUIRREL
PUBLISHING

Creating new Aisle locations

How to do it...

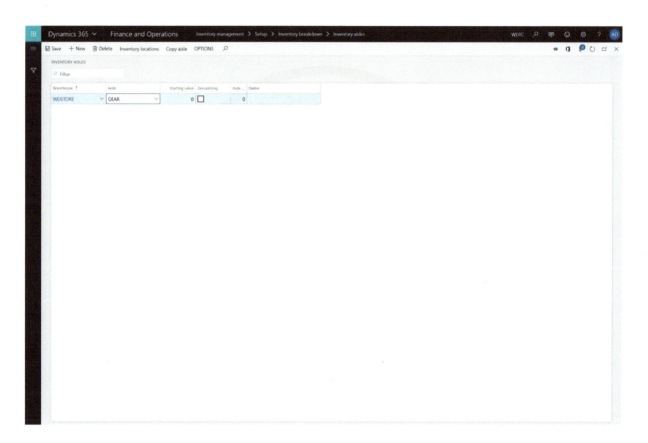

Step 3: Update the Aisle

Now we will be able to name our Aisle.

The first one that we will be setting up is for the general gear inventory.

To do this just change the **Aisle** value.

For this example, we will want to set the **Aisle** to **GEAR**.

Creating new Aisle locations

How to do it...

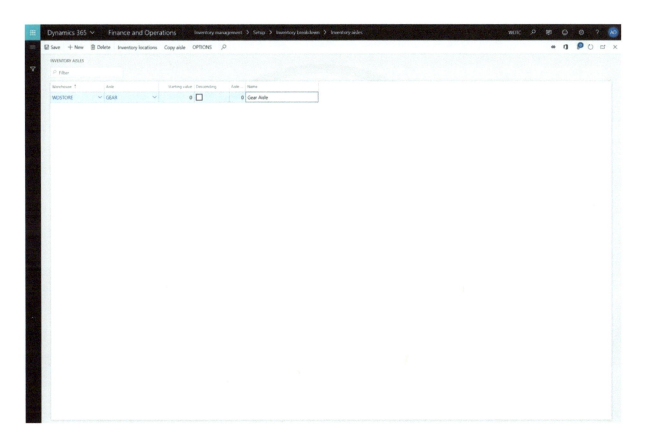

Step 4: Update the Name

And to finish off, we will want to give our aisle a more descriptive name.

To do this just change the **Name** value.

For this example, we will want to set the **Name** to **Gear Aisle**.

dync
dynamics companions
www.dynamicscompanions.com
Dynamics Companions

- 41 -

www.blindsquirrelpublishing.com
© 2019 Blind Squirrel Publishing, LLC , All Rights Reserved

BLIND SQUIRREL
PUBLISHING

Creating new Aisle locations

How to do it...

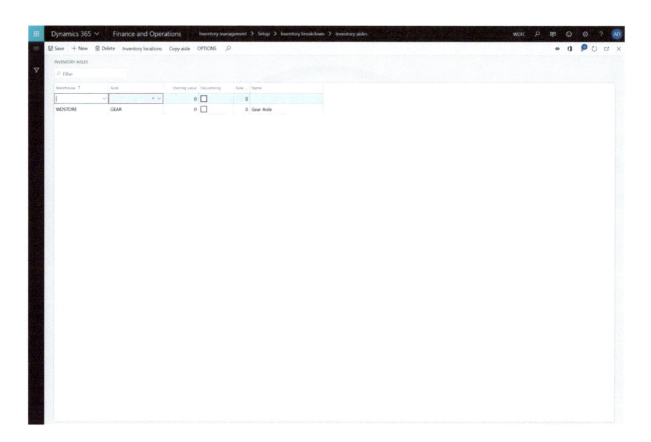

Step 5: Click on the New button

Let's continue on and set up some of the other aisles that we will manage within the warehouse.

To do this, all we need to do is click on the **New** button.

www.dynamicscompanions.com
Dynamics Companions

- 42 -

www.blindsquirrelpublishing.com
© 2019 Blind Squirrel Publishing, LLC , All Rights Reserved

BLIND SQUIRREL
PUBLISHING

Creating new Aisle locations

How to do it...

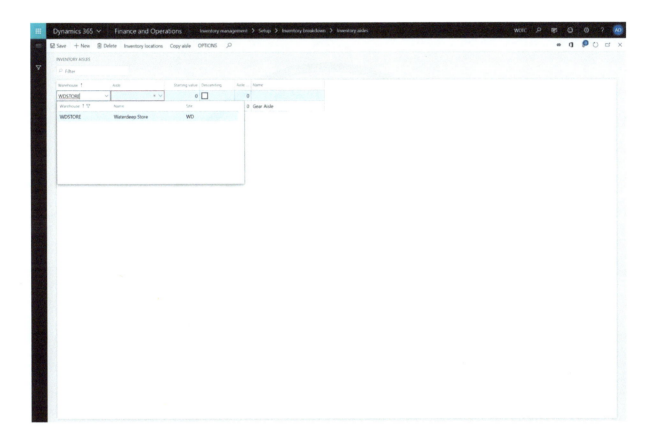

Step 6: Select the Warehouse

We will want to select our warehouse that the aisle will be associated with.

To do this just select the **Warehouse** option from the dropdown list.

This time, we will want to click on the **Warehouse** dropdown list and pick **WDSTORE**.

dync
dynamics companions

www.dynamicscompanions.com
Dynamics Companions

- 43 -

www.blindsquirrelpublishing.com
© 2019 Blind Squirrel Publishing, LLC , All Rights Reserved

BLIND SQUIRREL
PUBLISHING

Creating new Aisle locations

How to do it...

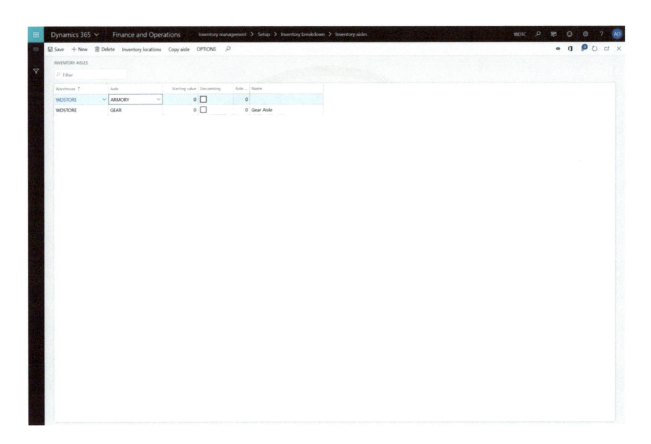

Step 7: Update the Aisle

We can now give our aisle a code that we will use to reference it.

To do this, we will just need to update the **Aisle** value.

For this example, we will want to set the **Aisle** to **ARMORY**.

dync
dynamics companions
www.dynamicscompanions.com
Dynamics Companions

- 44 -

www.blindsquirrelpublishing.com
© 2019 Blind Squirrel Publishing, LLC , All Rights Reserved

BLIND SQUIRREL
PUBLISHING

Creating new Aisle locations

How to do it...

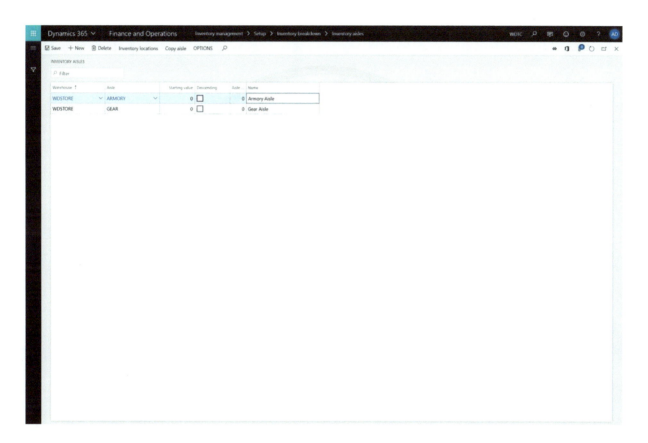

Step 8: Update the Name

And finally, we will give our aisle a more descriptive name.

To do this, we will just need to change the **Name** value.

For this example, we will want to set the **Name** to **Armory Aisle**.

dync
dynamics companions

www.dynamicscompanions.com
Dynamics Companions

- 45 -

www.blindsquirrelpublishing.com
© 2019 Blind Squirrel Publishing, LLC , All Rights Reserved

BLIND SQUIRREL
PUBLISHING

Creating new Aisle locations

How to do it...

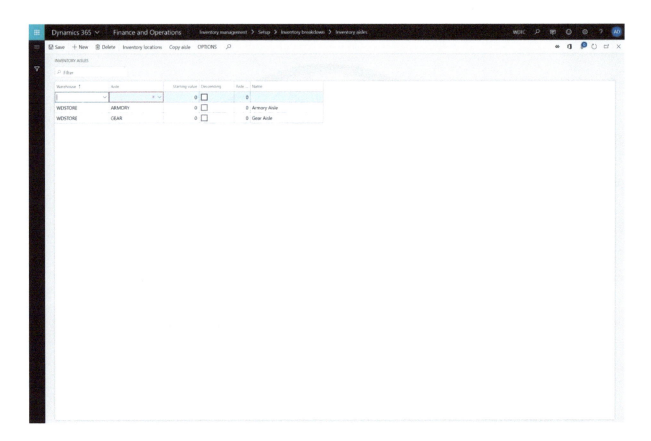

Step 9: Click on the New button

Let's add another aisle, for all of the books that we will be selling at the Waterdeep Trading Company store.

To do this just click on the **New** button.

www.dynamicscompanions.com
Dynamics Companions

- 46 -

www.blindsquirrelpublishing.com
© 2019 Blind Squirrel Publishing, LLC , All Rights Reserved

BLIND SQUIRREL
PUBLISHING

Creating new Aisle locations

How to do it...

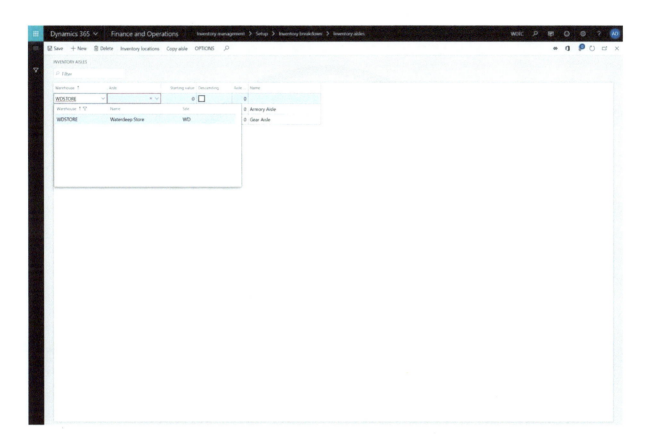

Step 10: Choose the Warehouse

We will want to select our warehouse again that we will be associating the aisle with.

To do this, we will just need to select the **Warehouse** value from the dropdown list.

For this example, we will want to click on the **Warehouse** dropdown list and select **WDSTORE**.

dync
dynamics companions
www.dynamicscompanions.com
Dynamics Companions

- 47 -

www.blindsquirrelpublishing.com
© 2019 Blind Squirrel Publishing, LLC , All Rights Reserved

BLIND SQUIRREL
PUBLISHING

Creating new Aisle locations

How to do it...

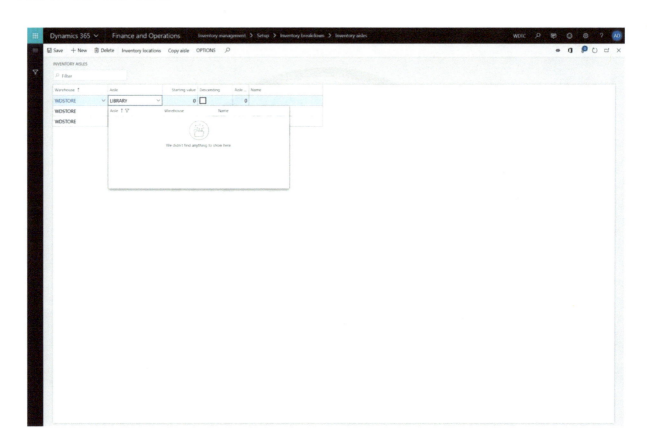

Step 11: Update the Aisle

Now we will assign our aisle a code to reference it by.

To do this just update the **Aisle** value.

This time, we will want to set the **Aisle** to **LIBRARY**.

dync
www.dynamicscompanions.com
Dynamics Companions

- 48 -

www.blindsquirrelpublishing.com
© 2019 Blind Squirrel Publishing, LLC , All Rights Reserved

BLIND SQUIRREL
PUBLISHING

Creating new Aisle locations

How to do it...

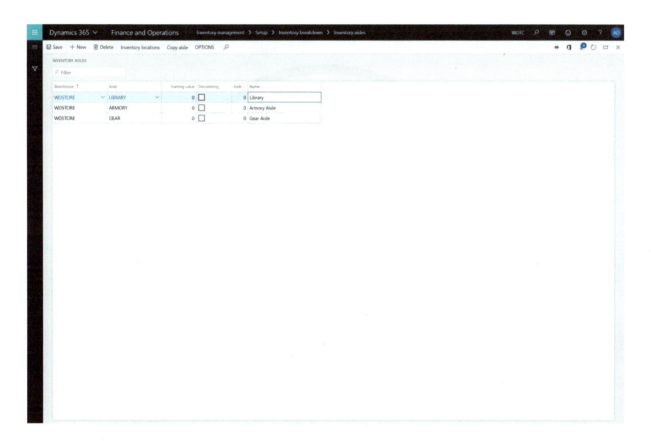

Step 12: Update the Name

And then we will add a more descriptive name to the aisle.

To do this just update the **Name** value.

This time, we will want to set the **Name** to **Library**.

dync
dynamics companion
www.dynamicscompanions.com
Dynamics Companions

- 49 -

www.blindsquirrelpublishing.com
© 2019 Blind Squirrel Publishing, LLC , All Rights Reserved

BLIND SQUIRREL
PUBLISHING

Creating new Aisle locations

How to do it...

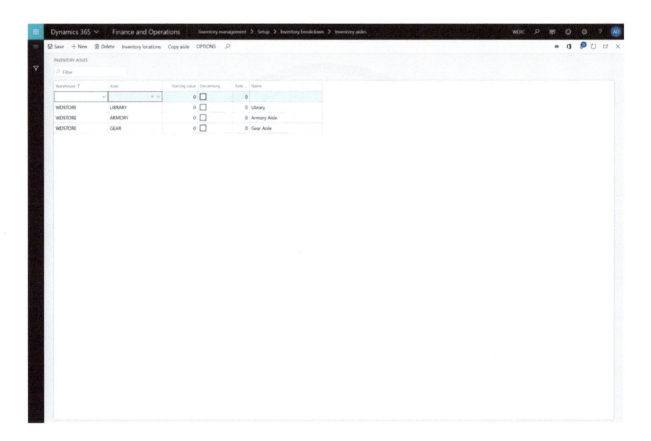

Step 13: Click on the New button

We will add a couple more aisle locations, and the next Aisle will be where we will store all of our ingredients and medications.

To do this, all we need to do is click on the **New** button.

dync
www.dynamicscompanions.com
Dynamics Companions

- 50 -

www.blindsquirrelpublishing.com
© 2019 Blind Squirrel Publishing, LLC , All Rights Reserved

BLIND SQUIRREL
PUBLISHING

Creating new Aisle locations

How to do it...

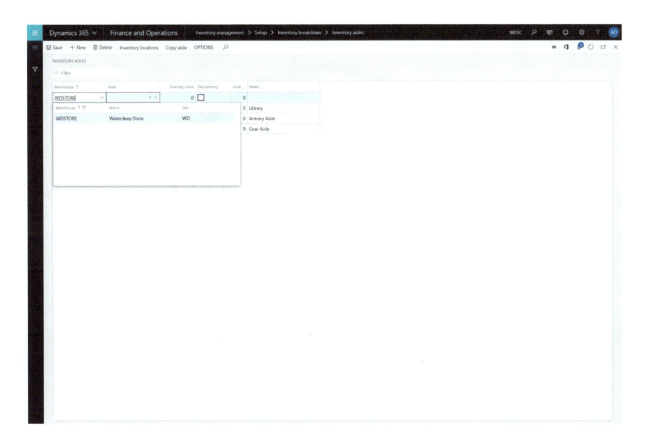

Step 14: Select the Warehouse

We will select our warehouse for the aisle.

To do this, we will just need to pick the **Warehouse** value from the dropdown list.

This time, we will want to click on the **Warehouse** dropdown list and pick **WDSTORE**.

dync
dynamics companions

www.dynamicscompanions.com
Dynamics Companions

- 51 -

www.blindsquirrelpublishing.com
© 2019 Blind Squirrel Publishing, LLC , All Rights Reserved

BLIND SQUIRREL
PUBLISHING

Creating new Aisle locations

How to do it...

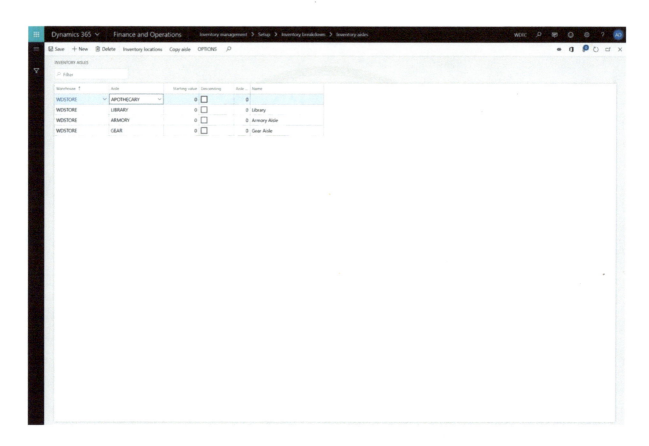

Step 15: Update the Aisle

We will give our aisle a code to reference it by.

To do this just update the **Aisle** value.

For this example, we will want to set the **Aisle** to **APOTHECARY**.

www.dynamicscompanions.com
Dynamics Companions

- 52 -

www.blindsquirrelpublishing.com
© 2019 Blind Squirrel Publishing, LLC , All Rights Reserved

BLIND SQUIRREL
PUBLISHING

Creating new Aisle locations

How to do it...

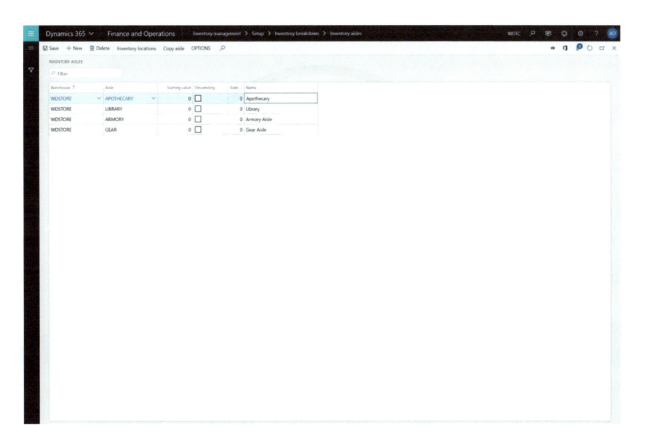

Step 16: Update the Name

And then we will give our apothecary aisle a more descriptive name.

To do this, we will just need to change the **Name** value.

This time, we will want to set the **Name** to **Apothecary**.

dync
dynamics companions

BLIND SQUIRREL
PUBLISHING

Creating new Aisle locations

How to do it...

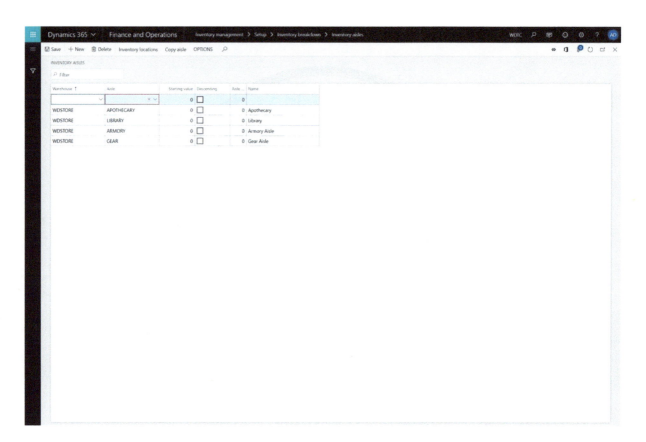

Step 17: Click on the New button

Let's add one last aisle to the warehouse, for the stables.

To do this just click on the **New** button.

dync
dynamics companions
www.dynamicscompanions.com
Dynamics Companions

- 54 -

www.blindsquirrelpublishing.com
© 2019 Blind Squirrel Publishing, LLC , All Rights Reserved

BLIND SQUIRREL
PUBLISHING

Creating new Aisle locations

How to do it...

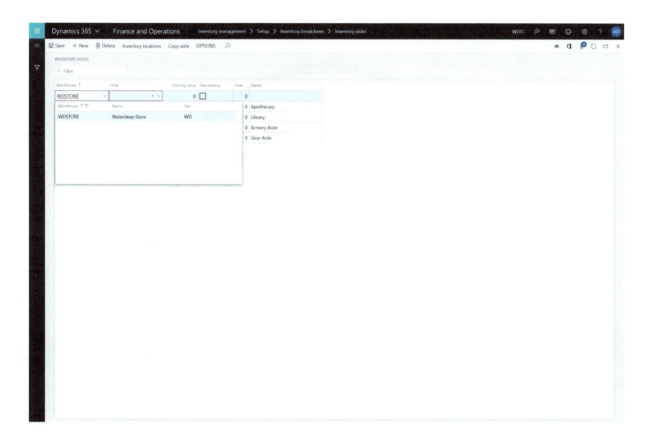

Step 18: Choose the Warehouse

Let's link this aisle to our warehouse.

To do this, we will just need to select the **Warehouse** value from the dropdown list.

For this example, we will want to click on the **Warehouse** dropdown list and select **WDSTORE**.

dync
dynamics companions
www.dynamicscompanions.com
Dynamics Companions

- 55 -

www.blindsquirrelpublishing.com
© 2019 Blind Squirrel Publishing, LLC , All Rights Reserved

BLIND SQUIRREL
PUBLISHING

Creating new Aisle locations

How to do it...

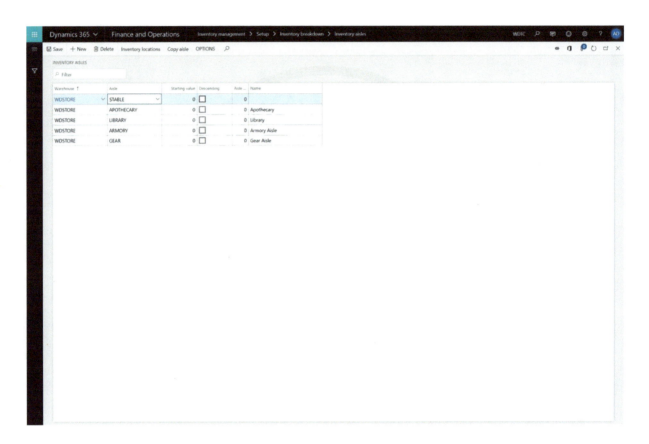

Step 19: Update the Aisle

We will then give our Stable aisle a code that we can identify it by.

To do this, we will just need to update the **Aisle** value.

This time, we will want to set the **Aisle** to **STABLE**.

dync
dynamics companions

www.dynamicscompanions.com
Dynamics Companions

- 56 -

www.blindsquirrelpublishing.com
© 2019 Blind Squirrel Publishing, LLC , All Rights Reserved

BLIND SQUIRREL
PUBLISHING

Creating new Aisle locations

How to do it...

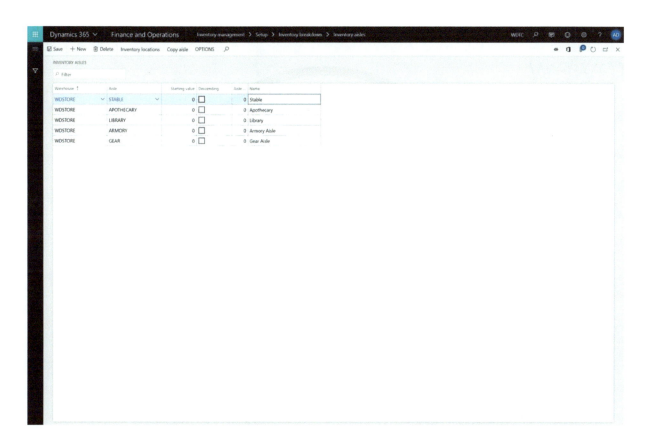

Step 20: Update the Name

And finally, we will give our aisle a proper name to accompany the code.

To do this, we will just need to update the **Name** value.

This time, we will want to set the **Name** to **Stable**.

dync
dynamics companions
www.dynamicscompanions.com
Dynamics Companions

- 57 -

www.blindsquirrelpublishing.com
© 2019 Blind Squirrel Publishing, LLC , All Rights Reserved

BLIND SQUIRREL
PUBLISHING

Review

Great. We now have all of the aisles that we will be setting up within our store warehouse. Let's move on.

Creating Locations within the Store Warehouse

Now that we have created our Aisle types, we can start to use them within the warehouse by creating different locations based on the aisles.

Topics Covered

- Opening the Inventory Locations maintenance form

- Creating new Inventory Locations

Opening the Inventory Locations maintenance form

To do this we will need to open up the **Inventory locations** maintenance form.

How to do it...

Step 1: Open the Inventory locations form through the menu search

We can find the **Inventory locations** form is through the menu search feature.

Type in **inventory loc** into the menu search and select **Inventory locations**.

Opening the Inventory Locations maintenance form

How to do it...

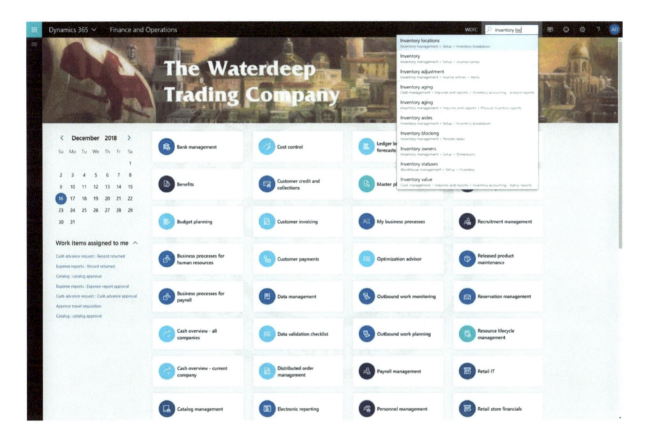

Step 1: Open the Inventory locations form through the menu search

We can find the **Inventory locations** form is through the menu search feature.

We can do this by clicking on the search icon in the header of the form (or by pressing **ALT+G**) and then type in **inventory loc** into the search box. Then you will be able to select the **Inventory locations** form from the dropdown list.

dync
dynamics companions
www.dynamicscompanions.com
Dynamics Companions

- 61 -

www.blindsquirrelpublishing.com
© 2019 Blind Squirrel Publishing, LLC , All Rights Reserved

BLIND SQUIRREL
PUBLISHING

Opening the Inventory Locations maintenance form

How to do it...

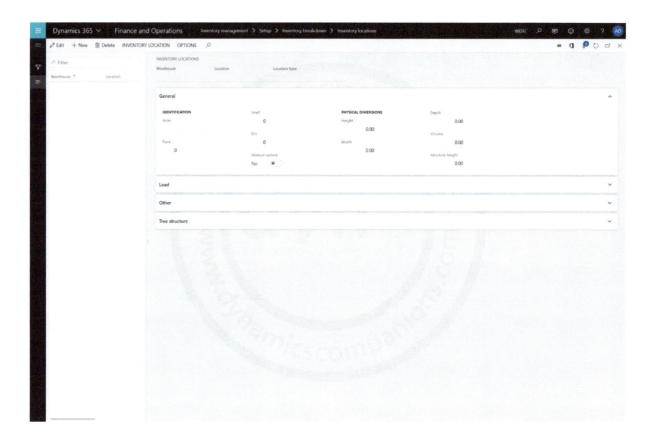

Step 1: Open the Inventory locations form through the menu search

This will open up the Inventory locations maintenance form which we will use to define all of the actual locations in the warehouse that we will be stocking our products.

dync
dynamics companions

www.dynamicscompanions.com
Dynamics Companions

- 62 -

www.blindsquirrelpublishing.com
© 2019 Blind Squirrel Publishing, LLC , All Rights Reserved

BLIND SQUIRREL
PUBLISHING

Creating new Inventory Locations

Now that we are in the Inventory locations maintenance form we can start to configure all of our locations.

How to do it...

Step 1: Click on the New button

We will start off by creating a new inventory location record.

Click on the **New** button.

Step 2: Select the Warehouse

We will want first to select the warehouse that we will be adding the inventory location to.

Click on the **Warehouse** dropdown list And choose **DWSTORE**.

Step 3: Choose the Location type

Next, we will want to select the type of inventory location this will be,

Click on the **Location type** dropdown list And choose **Picking location**.

Step 4: Choose the Aisle

Now we can select the aisle type from the list of aisles that we just configured in the previous step.

Click on the **Aisle** dropdown list And choose **GEAR**.

Step 5: Click on the New button

Let's continue on and set up the other inventory locations to match the other aisles that we set up.

Click on the **New** button.

Step 6: Choose the Warehouse

We will want to select our warehouse.

Click on the **Warehouse** dropdown list And choose **WDSTORE**.

Step 7: Choose the Location type

Let's set the type of inventory location to be a picking location.

Click on the **Location type** dropdown list And select **Picking location**.

Step 8: Select the Aisle

And then we can select the aisle type.

Click on the **Aisle** dropdown list And choose **ARMORY**.

Step 9: Click on the New button

We will continue on and set up some more inventory locations.

Click on the **New** button.

 www.dynamicscompanions.com
Dynamics Companions

- 63 -

 www.blindsquirrelpublishing.com
© 2019 Blind Squirrel Publishing, LLC , All Rights Reserved

 BLIND SQUIRREL
PUBLISHING

Step 10: Choose the Warehouse

Just like before we will want to select our warehouse.

Click on the **Warehouse** dropdown list And choose **WDSTORE**.

Step 11: Select the Location type

We will want this location to be a picking location.

Click on the **Location type** dropdown list And select **Picking location**.

Step 12: Choose the Aisle

And then we can select the library aisle type.

Click on the **Aisle** dropdown list And choose **LIBRARY**.

Step 13: Click on the New button

We're halfway through, so let's continue on and add another inventory location for the apothecary area in the warehouse.

Click on the **New** button.

Step 14: Select the Warehouse

We will want to link this to the warehouse that we have for the store.

Click on the **Warehouse** dropdown list And choose **WDSTORE**.

Step 15: Select the Location type

We will want to mark this inventory location as a picking location.

Click on the **Location type** dropdown list And select **Picking location**.

Step 16: Select the Aisle

And then we will want to select the aisle type from the list of aisles.

Click on the **Aisle** dropdown list And select **APOTHECARY**.

Step 17: Click on the New button

Let's finish off by adding the last inventory location which will be for the stables.

Click on the **New** button.

Step 18: Choose the Warehouse

Let's select the warehouse that we will link the inventory location to.

Click on the **Warehouse** dropdown list And choose **WDSTORE**.

Step 19: Choose the Location type

We will want to mark this inventory location as being a picking location.

Click on the **Location type** dropdown list And choose **Picking location**.

Step 20: Select the Aisle

And then we will want to select the Stable aisle from the list of aisles that we set up earlier on.

Click on the **Aisle** dropdown list And select **STABLE**.

Step 21: Click on the Save button

After we have done that we can just save the updates and we are done.

Click on the **Save** button.

Creating new Inventory Locations

How to do it...

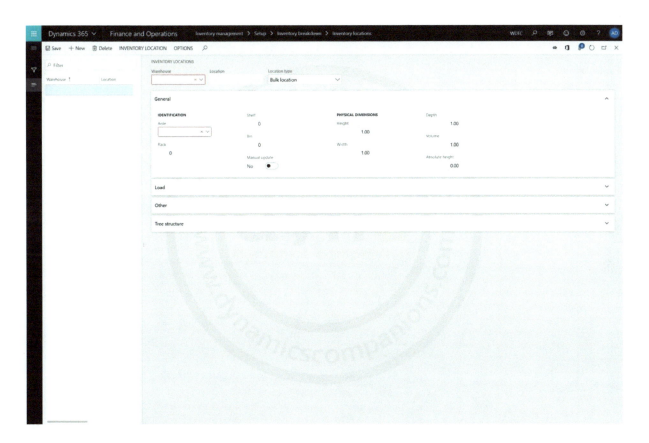

Step 1: Click on the New button

We will start off by creating a new inventory location record.

To do this just click on the **New** button.

www.dynamicscompanions.com
Dynamics Companions

- 65 -

www.blindsquirrelpublishing.com
© 2019 Blind Squirrel Publishing, LLC , All Rights Reserved

BLIND SQUIRREL
PUBLISHING

Creating new Inventory Locations

How to do it...

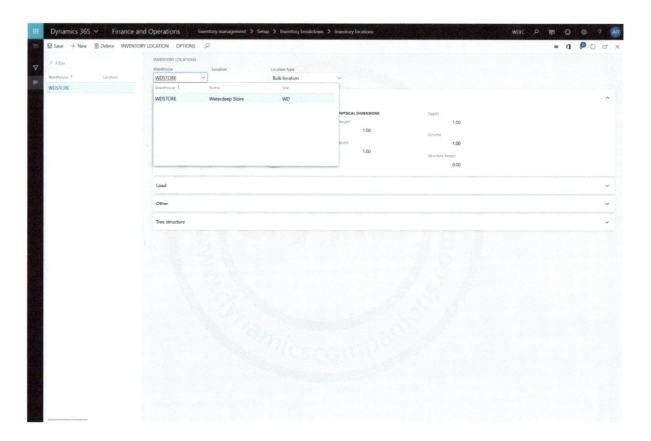

Step 2: Select the Warehouse

We will want first to select the warehouse that we will be adding the inventory location to.

To do this just select the **Warehouse** value from the dropdown list.

This time, we will want to click on the **Warehouse** dropdown list and pick **DWSTORE**.

dync
www.dynamicscompanions.com
Dynamics Companions

- 66 -

www.blindsquirrelpublishing.com
© 2019 Blind Squirrel Publishing, LLC , All Rights Reserved

BLIND SQUIRREL
PUBLISHING

Creating new Inventory Locations

How to do it...

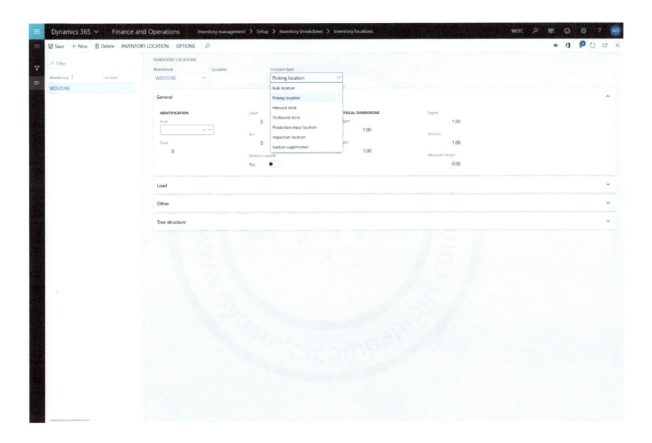

Step 3: Choose the Location type

Next, we will want to select the type of inventory location this will be,

To do this, we will just need to pick the **Location type** value from the dropdown list.

For this example, we will want to click on the **Location type** dropdown list and pick **Picking location**.

dync
dynamics companions

www.dynamicscompanions.com
Dynamics Companions

- 67 -

www.blindsquirrelpublishing.com
© 2019 Blind Squirrel Publishing, LLC , All Rights Reserved

BLIND SQUIRREL
PUBLISHING

Creating new Inventory Locations

How to do it...

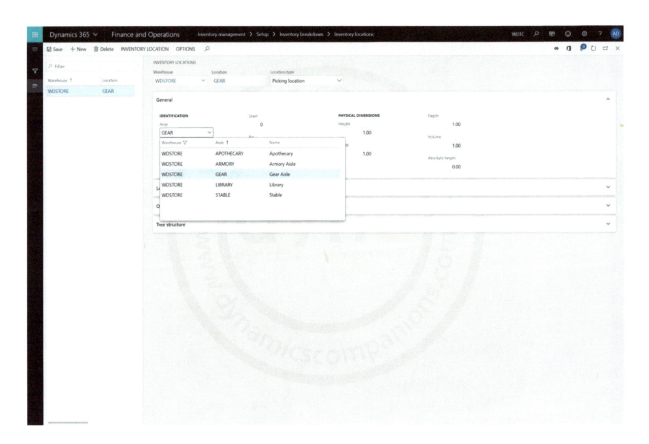

Step 4: Choose the Aisle

Now we can select the aisle type from the list of aisles that we just configured in the previous step.

To do this just select the **Aisle** option from the dropdown list.

For this example, we will want to click on the **Aisle** dropdown list and pick **GEAR**.

www.dynamicscompanions.com
Dynamics Companions

- 68 -

www.blindsquirrelpublishing.com
© 2019 Blind Squirrel Publishing, LLC , All Rights Reserved

BLIND SQUIRREL
PUBLISHING

Creating new Inventory Locations

How to do it...

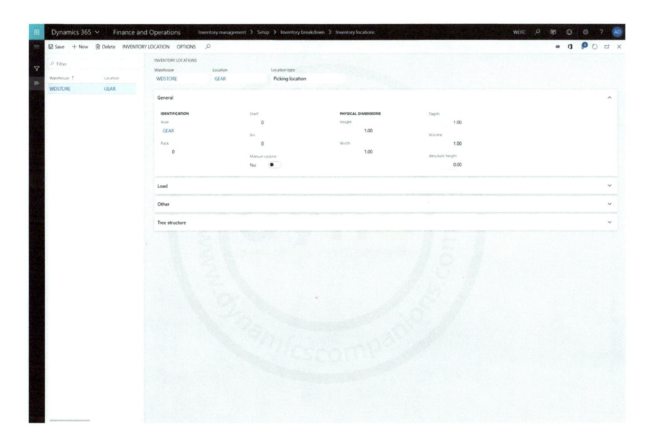

Step 4: Choose the Aisle

After we have done that we are done setting up our first inventory location.

dync
dynamics companions
www.dynamicscompanions.com
Dynamics Companions

- 69 -

www.blindsquirrelpublishing.com
© 2019 Blind Squirrel Publishing, LLC, All Rights Reserved

BLIND SQUIRREL
PUBLISHING

Creating new Inventory Locations

How to do it...

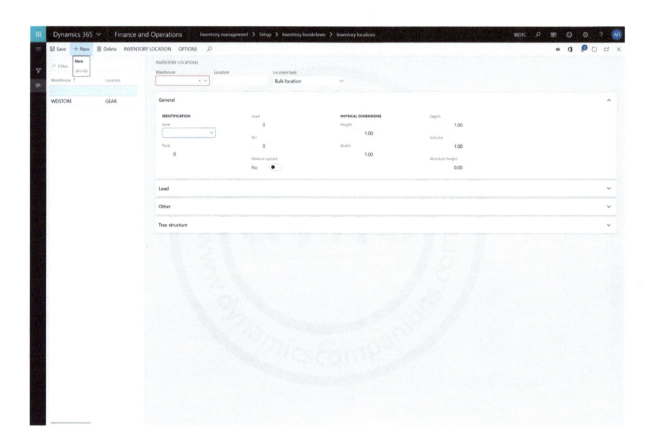

Step 5: Click on the New button

Let's continue on and set up the other inventory locations to match the other aisles that we set up.

To do this, all we need to do is click on the **New** button.

dync
www.dynamicscompanions.com
Dynamics Companions

- 70 -

www.blindsquirrelpublishing.com
© 2019 Blind Squirrel Publishing, LLC , All Rights Reserved

BLIND SQUIRREL
PUBLISHING

Creating new Inventory Locations

How to do it...

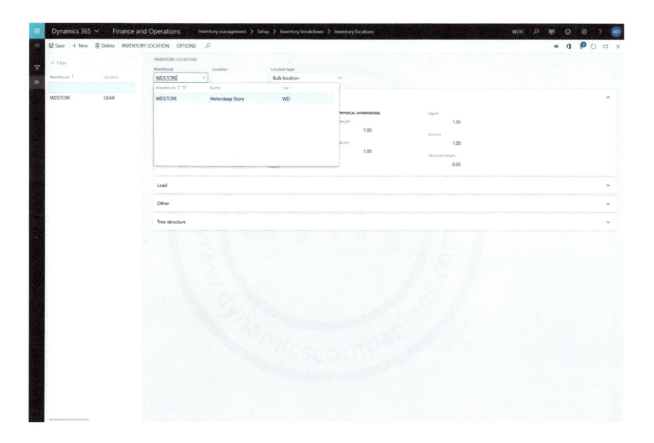

Step 6: Choose the Warehouse

We will want to select our warehouse.

To do this just pick the **Warehouse** option from the dropdown list.

For this example, we will want to click on the **Warehouse** dropdown list and select **WDSTORE**.

dync
dynamics companions

www.dynamicscompanions.com
Dynamics Companions

- 71 -

www.blindsquirrelpublishing.com
© 2019 Blind Squirrel Publishing, LLC , All Rights Reserved

BLIND SQUIRREL
PUBLISHING

Creating new Inventory Locations

How to do it...

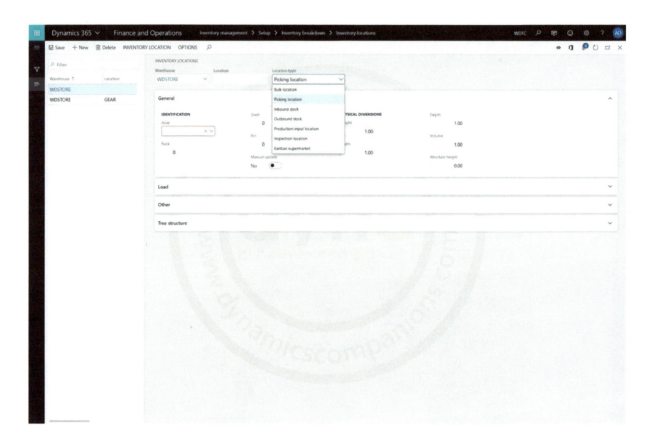

Step 7: Choose the Location type

Let's set the type of inventory location to be a picking location.

To do this just select the **Location type** option from the dropdown list.

For this example, we will want to click on the **Location type** dropdown list and pick **Picking location**.

dyn c
dynamics companions
www.dynamicscompanions.com
Dynamics Companions

- 72 -

www.blindsquirrelpublishing.com
© 2019 Blind Squirrel Publishing, LLC , All Rights Reserved

BLIND SQUIRREL
PUBLISHING

Creating new Inventory Locations

How to do it...

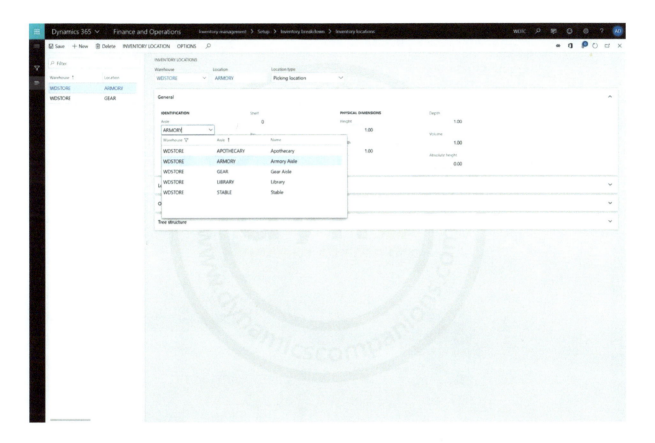

Step 8: Select the Aisle

And then we can select the aisle type.

To do this, we will just need to pick the **Aisle** value from the dropdown list.

This time, we will want to click on the **Aisle** dropdown list and select **ARMORY**.

dync
dynamics companions

www.dynamicscompanions.com
Dynamics Companions

- 73 -

www.blindsquirrelpublishing.com
© 2019 Blind Squirrel Publishing, LLC , All Rights Reserved

BLIND SQUIRREL
PUBLISHING

Creating new Inventory Locations

How to do it...

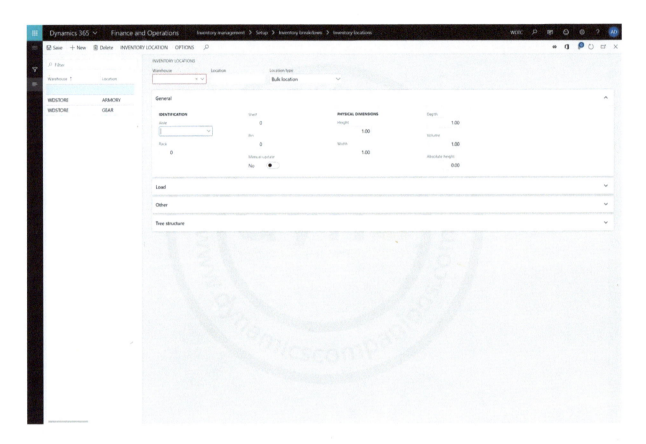

Step 9: Click on the New button

We will continue on and set up some more inventory locations.

To do this, all we need to do is click on the **New** button.

dync
www.dynamicscompanions.com
Dynamics Companions

- 74 -

www.blindsquirrelpublishing.com
© 2019 Blind Squirrel Publishing, LLC , All Rights Reserved

BLIND SQUIRREL
PUBLISHING

Creating new Inventory Locations

How to do it...

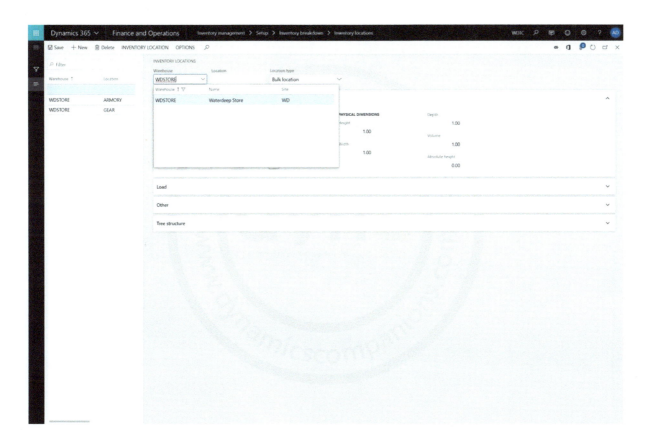

Step 10: Choose the Warehouse

Just like before we will want to select our warehouse.

To do this just pick the **Warehouse** option from the dropdown list.

For this example, we will want to click on the **Warehouse** dropdown list and select **WDSTORE**.

Creating new Inventory Locations

How to do it...

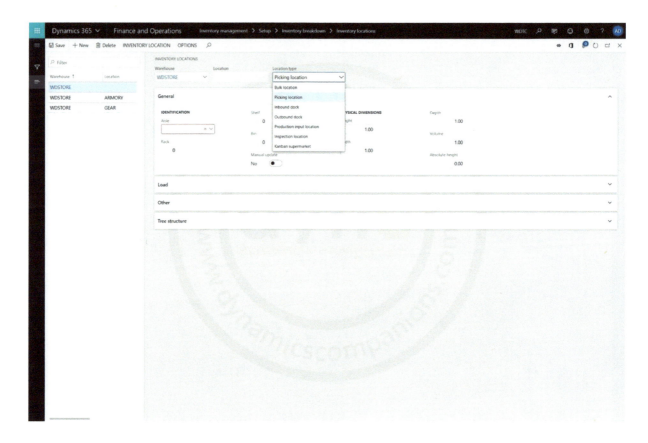

Step 11: Select the Location type

We will want this location to be a picking location.

To do this just pick the **Location type** value from the dropdown list.

For this example, we will want to click on the **Location type** dropdown list and pick **Picking location**.

dyn c
dynamics companions

www.dynamicscompanions.com
Dynamics Companions

- 76 -

www.blindsquirrelpublishing.com
© 2019 Blind Squirrel Publishing, LLC , All Rights Reserved

BLIND SQUIRREL
PUBLISHING

Creating new Inventory Locations

How to do it...

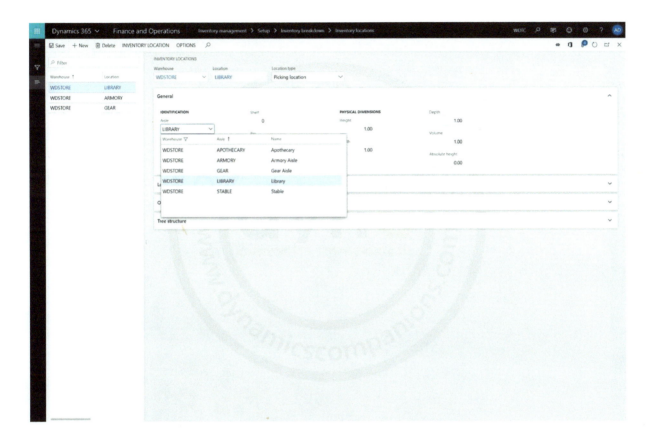

Step 12: Choose the Aisle

And then we can select the library aisle type.

To do this just select the **Aisle** option from the dropdown list.

For this example, we will want to click on the **Aisle** dropdown list and pick **LIBRARY**.

dync
dynamics companions

www.dynamicscompanions.com
Dynamics Companions

- 77 -

www.blindsquirrelpublishing.com
© 2019 Blind Squirrel Publishing, LLC , All Rights Reserved

BLIND SQUIRREL
PUBLISHING

Creating new Inventory Locations

How to do it...

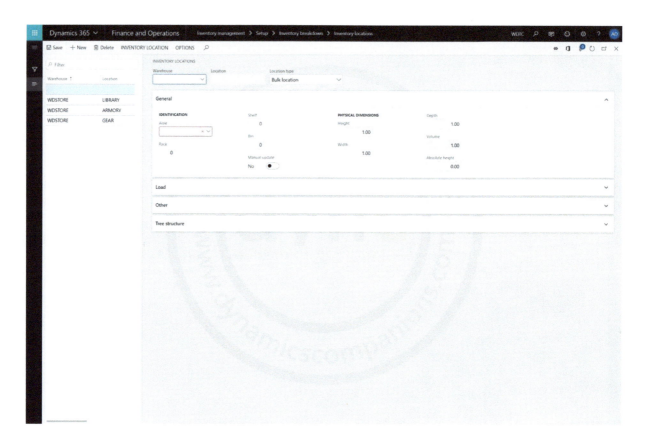

Step 13: Click on the New button

We're halfway through, so let's continue on and add another inventory location for the apothecary area in the warehouse.

To do this just click on the **New** button.

www.dynamicscompanions.com
Dynamics Companions

- 78 -

www.blindsquirrelpublishing.com
© 2019 Blind Squirrel Publishing, LLC, All Rights Reserved

BLIND SQUIRREL
PUBLISHING

Creating new Inventory Locations

How to do it...

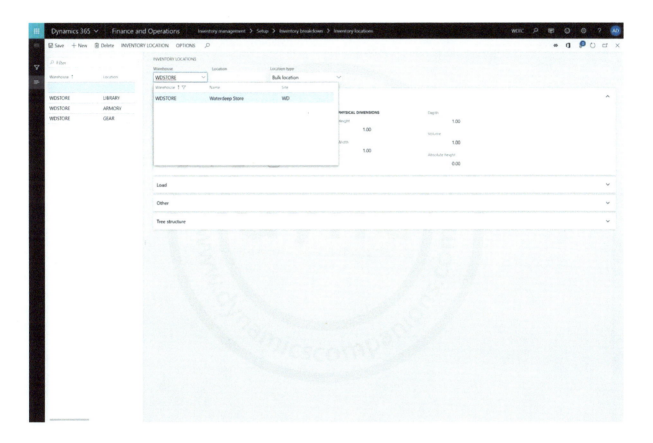

Step 14: Select the Warehouse

We will want to link this to the warehouse that we have for the store.

To do this just select the **Warehouse** value from the dropdown list.

This time, we will want to click on the **Warehouse** dropdown list and select **WDSTORE**.

dync
dynamics companions

www.dynamicscompanions.com
Dynamics Companions

- 79 -

www.blindsquirrelpublishing.com
© 2019 Blind Squirrel Publishing, LLC , All Rights Reserved

BLIND SQUIRREL
PUBLISHING

Creating new Inventory Locations

How to do it...

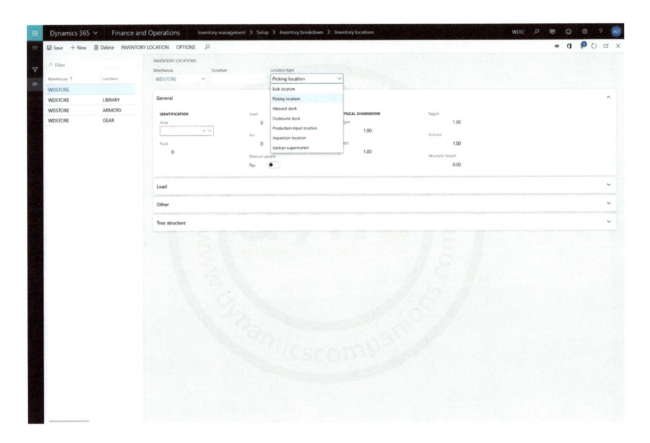

Step 15: Select the Location type

We will want to mark this inventory location as a picking location.

To do this, we will just need to pick the **Location type** value from the dropdown list.

This time, we will want to click on the **Location type** dropdown list and select **Picking location**.

www.blindsquirrelpublishing.com
© 2019 Blind Squirrel Publishing, LLC , All Rights Reserved

BLIND SQUIRREL
PUBLISHING

Creating new Inventory Locations

How to do it...

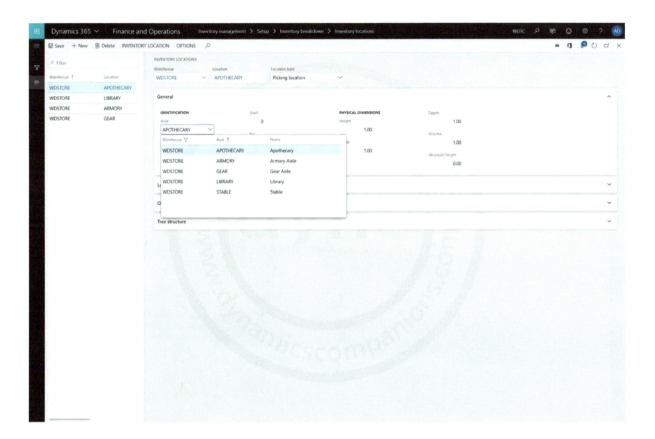

Step 16: Select the Aisle

And then we will want to select the aisle type from the list of aisles.

To do this, we will just need to pick the **Aisle** value from the dropdown list.

For this example, we will want to click on the **Aisle** dropdown list and select **APOTHECARY**.

dync
dynamics companions
www.dynamicscompanions.com
Dynamics Companions
- 81 -
www.blindsquirrelpublishing.com
© 2019 Blind Squirrel Publishing, LLC , All Rights Reserved
BLIND SQUIRREL
PUBLISHING

Creating new Inventory Locations

How to do it...

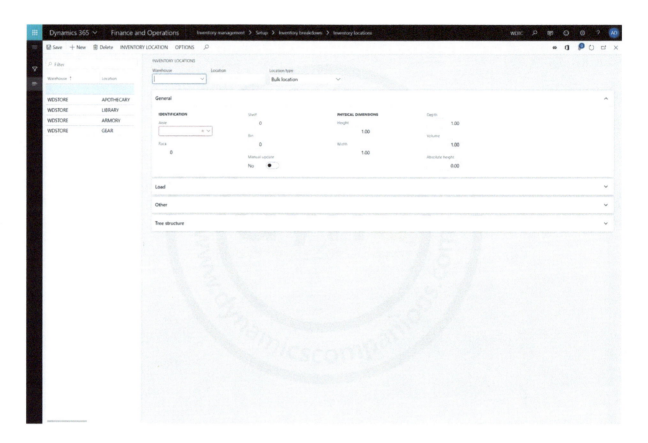

Step 17: Click on the New button

Let's finish off by adding the last inventory location which will be for the stables.

To do this just click on the **New** button.

dync
dynamics companions
www.dynamicscompanions.com
Dynamics Companions
- 82 -
www.blindsquirrelpublishing.com
© 2019 Blind Squirrel Publishing, LLC , All Rights Reserved
BLIND SQUIRREL
PUBLISHING

Creating new Inventory Locations

How to do it...

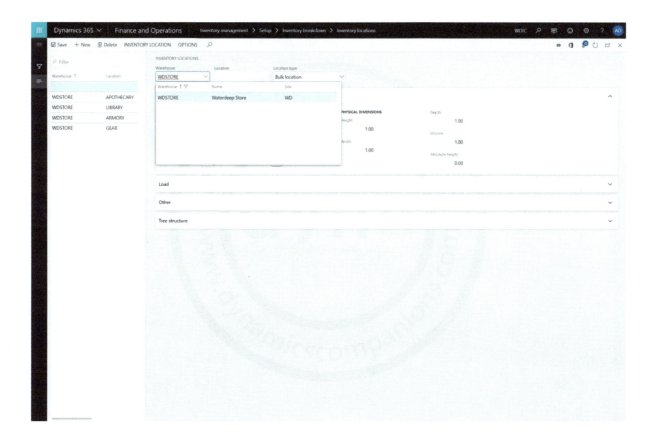

Step 18: Choose the Warehouse

Let's select the warehouse that we will link the inventory location to.

To do this just select the **Warehouse** value from the dropdown list.

This time, we will want to click on the **Warehouse** dropdown list and pick **WDSTORE**.

www.dynamicscompanions.com
Dynamics Companions

- 83 -

www.blindsquirrelpublishing.com
© 2019 Blind Squirrel Publishing, LLC , All Rights Reserved

BLIND SQUIRREL
PUBLISHING

Creating new Inventory Locations

How to do it...

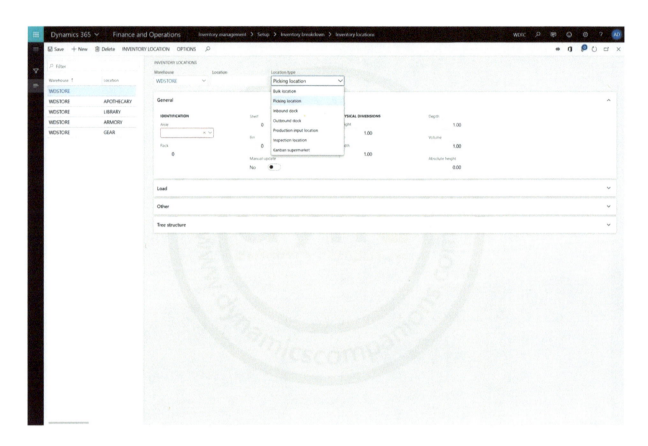

Step 19: Choose the Location type

We will want to mark this inventory location as being a picking location.

To do this just pick the **Location type** option from the dropdown list.

For this example, we will want to click on the **Location type** dropdown list and pick **Picking location**.

Creating new Inventory Locations

How to do it...

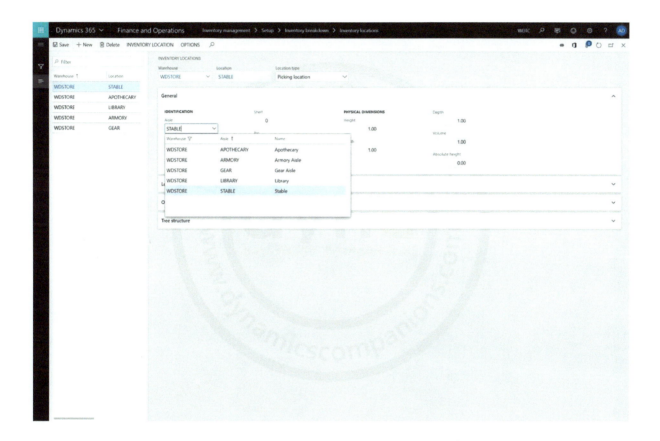

Step 20: Select the Aisle

And then we will want to select the Stable aisle from the list of aisles that we set up earlier on.

To do this just select the **Aisle** option from the dropdown list.

This time, we will want to click on the **Aisle** dropdown list and select **STABLE**.

dync
dynamics companion

www.dynamicscompanions.com
Dynamics Companions

- 85 -

www.blindsquirrelpublishing.com
© 2019 Blind Squirrel Publishing, LLC , All Rights Reserved

BLIND SQUIRREL
PUBLISHING

Creating new Inventory Locations

How to do it...

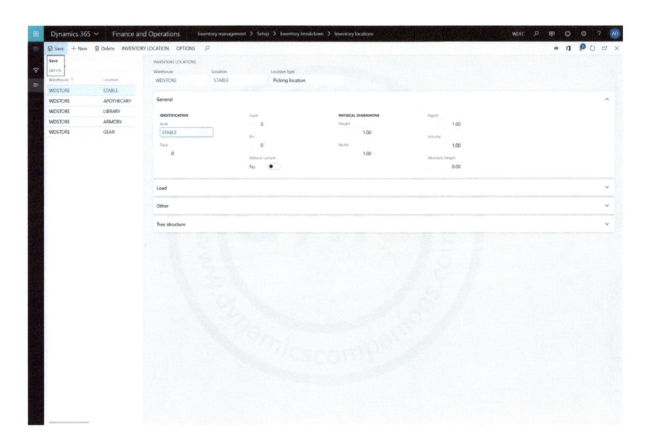

Step 21: Click on the Save button

After we have done that we can just save the updates and we are done.

To do this, all we need to do is click on the **Save** button.

dync
www.dynamicscompanions.com
Dynamics Companions

- 86 -

www.blindsquirrelpublishing.com
© 2019 Blind Squirrel Publishing, LLC , All Rights Reserved

BLIND SQUIRREL
PUBLISHING

Review

How easy was that? We just set up a number of new inventory locations within the warehouse based on the aisle types that we defined in the system.

www.blindsquirrelpublishing.com
© 2019 Blind Squirrel Publishing, LLC , All Rights Reserved

Summary

Congratulations. We have now set up our first warehouse for the **Waterdeep Trading Company**, and also organized the inventory locations based on the warehouse layout.

Configuring Products

Now that we have our warehouse configured, we can move on to the creation of the product records that we will use to track all of the inventory and transactions by.

Topics Covered

- Creating An Item Model Group

- Creating An Item Group

- Adding a New Product

Creating An Item Model Group

Before we can create our products though there are a couple of configuration codes that we will need to set up for the products. The first will be an **Item model group** which will help us manage the product.

Topics Covered

- Opening the Item Model Group maintenance form
- Creating a new Item Model Group

Opening the Item Model Group maintenance form

To do this we will want to find the **Item model group** maintenance form.

How to do it...

Step 1: Open the Item model group form through the menu search

We can find the **Item model group** form is through the menu search feature.

Type in **item mod** into the menu search and select **Item model group**.

Opening the Item Model Group maintenance form

How to do it...

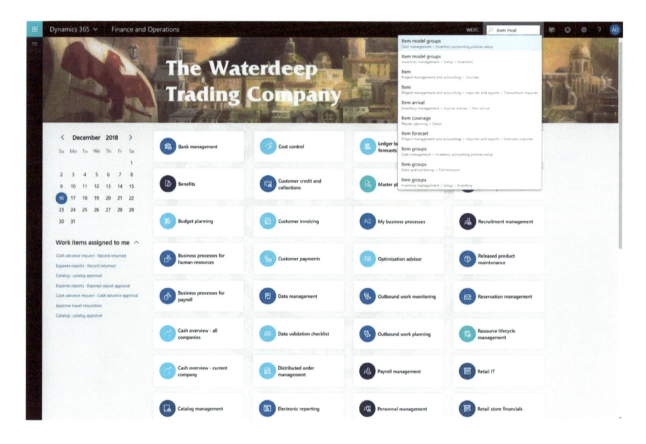

Step 1: Open the Item model group form through the menu search

We can find the **Item model group** form is through the menu search feature.

We can do this by clicking on the search icon in the header of the form (or by pressing **ALT+G**) and then type in **item mod** into the search box. Then you will be able to select the **Item model group** form from the dropdown list.

dyn c
dynamics companions

www.dynamicscompanions.com
Dynamics Companions

- 92 -

www.blindsquirrelpublishing.com
© 2019 Blind Squirrel Publishing, LLC , All Rights Reserved

BLIND SQUIRREL
PUBLISHING

Opening the Item Model Group maintenance form

How to do it...

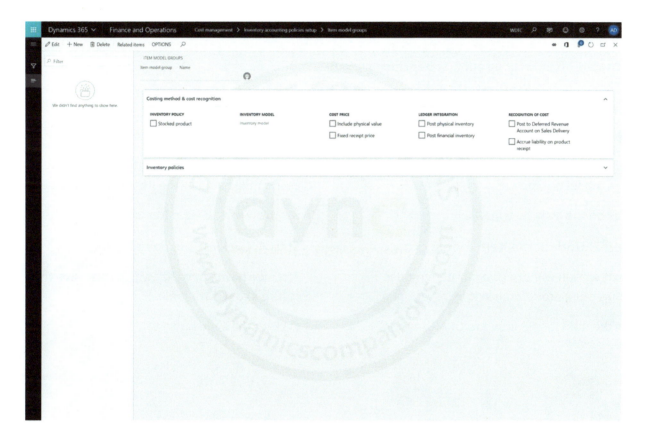

Step 1: Open the Item model group form through the menu search

This will open up the Item model group maintenance form where we will be able to set up our Item model groups.

www.dynamicscompanions.com
Dynamics Companions

- 93 -

www.blindsquirrelpublishing.com
© 2019 Blind Squirrel Publishing, LLC , All Rights Reserved

BLIND SQUIRREL
PUBLISHING

Creating a new Item Model Group

Let's start off by creating our first Item model group.

How to do it...

Step 1: Click on the New button

We will want to create a new record for our Item model group.

Click on the **New** button.

Step 2: Update the Item model group

Next, we will want to give our Item model group a code to reference it by.

Set the Item model group to GEAR.

Step 3: Update the Name

And then we will want to add a more descriptive name to the Item model group.

Set the Name to Gear Items.

Step 4: Click on the Save button

After we have done that we can just save the record and we are done.

Click on the **Save** button.

Creating a new Item Model Group

How to do it...

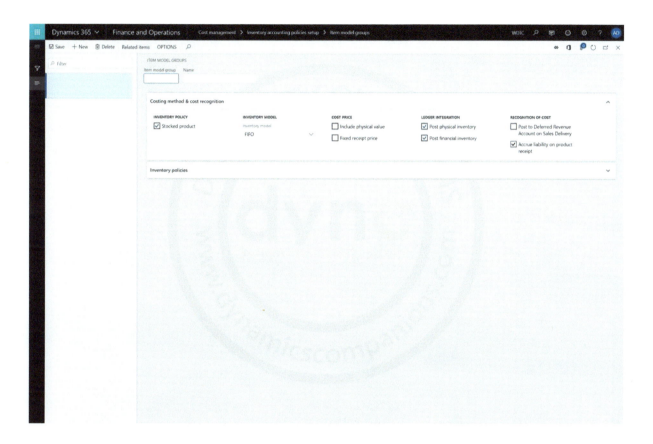

Step 1: Click on the New button

We will want to create a new record for our Item model group.

To do this just click on the **New** button.

dync
dynamics companions

www.dynamicscompanions.com
Dynamics Companions

www.blindsquirrelpublishing.com
© 2019 Blind Squirrel Publishing, LLC , All Rights Reserved

BLIND SQUIRREL
PUBLISHING

Creating a new Item Model Group

How to do it...

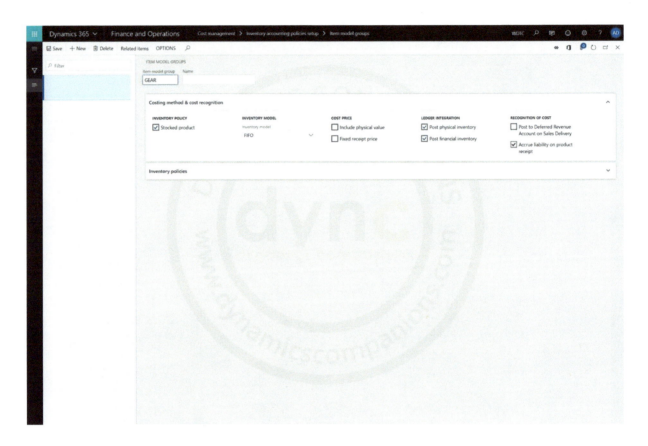

Step 2: Update the Item model group

Next, we will want to give our Item model group a code to reference it by.

To do this, we will just need to change the **Item model group** value.

For this example, we will want to set the **Item model group** to **GEAR**.

dync
dynamics companions

BLIND SQUIRREL
PUBLISHING

Creating a new Item Model Group

How to do it...

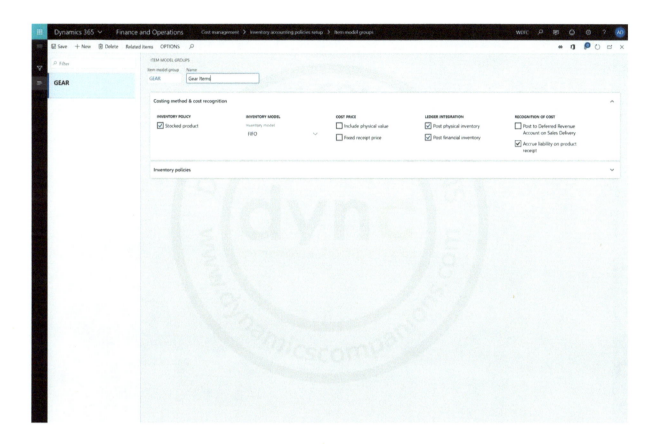

Step 3: Update the Name

And then we will want to add a more descriptive name to the Item model group.

To do this just update the **Name** value.

This time, we will want to set the **Name** to **Gear Items**.

dync
dynamics companions
www.dynamicscompanions.com
Dynamics Companions

- 97 -

www.blindsquirrelpublishing.com
© 2019 Blind Squirrel Publishing, LLC , All Rights Reserved

BLIND SQUIRREL
PUBLISHING

Creating a new Item Model Group

How to do it...

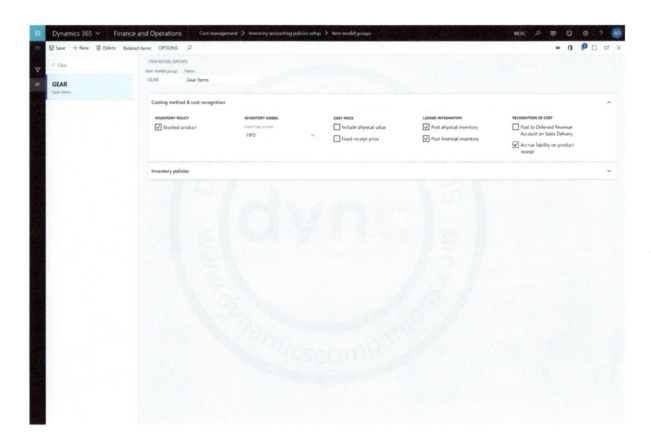

Step 4: Click on the Save button

After we have done that we can just save the record and we are done.

To do this, all we need to do is click on the **Save** button.

dync
dynamics companions

www.dynamicscompanions.com
Dynamics Companions

- 98 -

www.blindsquirrelpublishing.com
© 2019 Blind Squirrel Publishing, LLC , All Rights Reserved

BLIND SQUIRREL
PUBLISHING

Review

How easy was that? We now have item model groups that we will need later on in the setup of our products.

Creating An Item Group

The other inventory control that we will need to set up is for the Item groups, which we will associate with the products and it will give us our default posting information.

Topics Covered

- Opening the Item Group maintenance form

- Adding a new Item Group

Opening the Item Group maintenance form

In order to do this we will need to find the Item group maintenance form.

How to do it...

Step 1: Open the Item groups form through the menu search

We can find the **Item groups** form through the menu search feature.

Type in **item groups** into the menu search and select **Item groups**.

dync
dynamics companions

www.dynamicscompanions.com
Dynamics Companions

- 101 -

www.blindsquirrelpublishing.com
© 2019 Blind Squirrel Publishing, LLC , All Rights Reserved

BLIND SQUIRREL
PUBLISHING

Opening the Item Group maintenance form

How to do it...

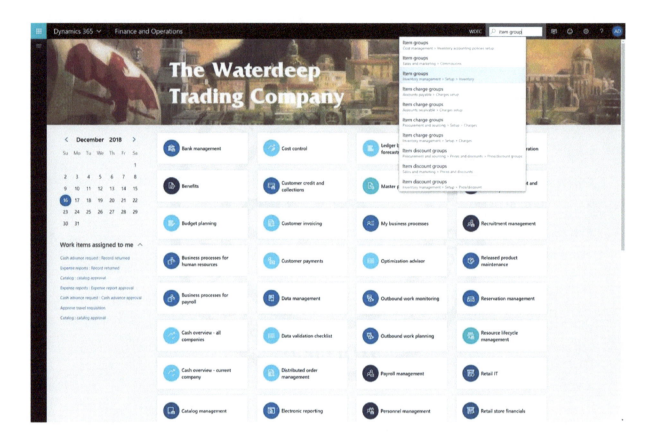

Step 1: Open the Item groups form through the menu search

We can find the **Item groups** form through the menu search feature.

We can do this by clicking on the search icon in the header of the form (or by pressing **ALT+G**) and then type in **item groups** into the search box. Then you will be able to select the **Item groups** form from the dropdown list.

dync
www.dynamicscompanions.com
Dynamics Companions

- 102 -

www.blindsquirrelpublishing.com
© 2019 Blind Squirrel Publishing, LLC, All Rights Reserved

BLIND SQUIRREL
PUBLISHING

Opening the Item Group maintenance form

How to do it...

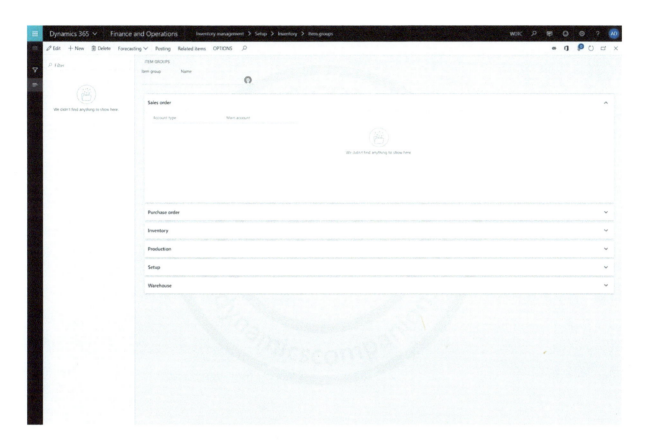

Step 1: Open the Item groups form through the menu search

This will open up the Item groups maintenance form where we will be able to define the different item groups and their posting profiles.

dync
dynamics companions
www.dynamicscompanions.com
Dynamics Companions

- 103 -

www.blindsquirrelpublishing.com
© 2019 Blind Squirrel Publishing, LLC , All Rights Reserved

BLIND SQUIRREL
PUBLISHING

Adding a new Item Group

Now we will want to add our first Item group into the system.

How to do it...

Step 1: Click on the New button

We will start off by creating a new Item group record.

Click on the **New** button.

Step 2: Update the Item group

We will then give our item group a code to reference it by.

Set the Item group to GEAR.

Step 3: Update the Name

And then we can add a more descriptive name for the item group.

Set the **Name** to **Gear**.

Step 4: Click on the Save button

After we have done that we can save the record.

Click on the **Save** button.

Adding a new Item Group

How to do it...

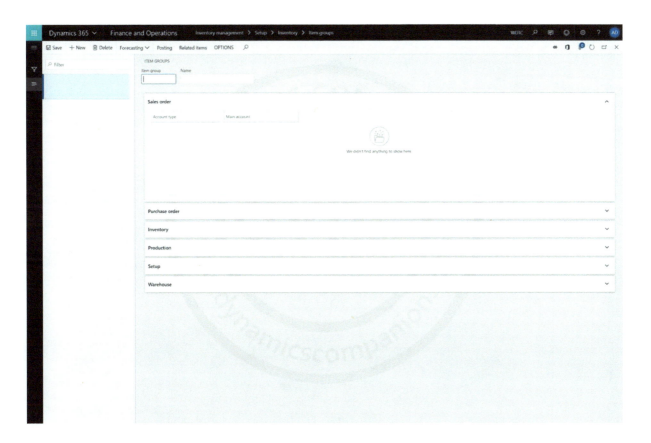

Step 1: Click on the New button

We will start off by creating a new Item group record.

To do this, all we need to do is click on the **New** button.

www.dynamicscompanions.com
Dynamics Companions

- 105 -

www.blindsquirrelpublishing.com
© 2019 Blind Squirrel Publishing, LLC , All Rights Reserved

BLIND SQUIRREL
PUBLISHING

Adding a new Item Group

How to do it...

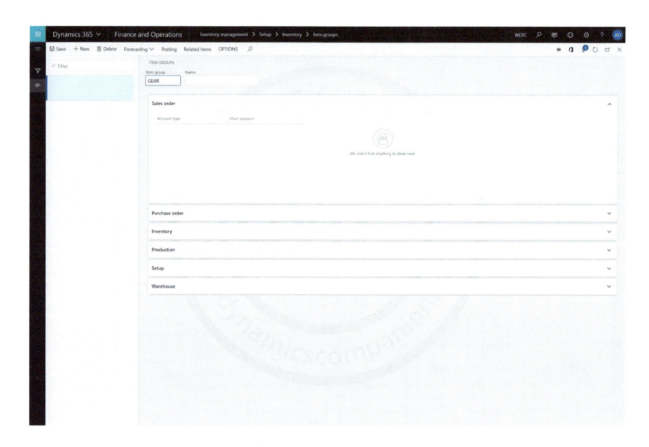

Step 2: Update the Item group

We will then give our item group a code to reference it by.

To do this, we will just need to update the **Item group** value.

This time, we will want to set the **Item group** to **GEAR**.

dync
dynamics companions

www.dynamicscompanions.com
Dynamics Companions

- 106 -

www.blindsquirrelpublishing.com
© 2019 Blind Squirrel Publishing, LLC , All Rights Reserved

BLIND SQUIRREL
PUBLISHING

Adding a new Item Group

How to do it...

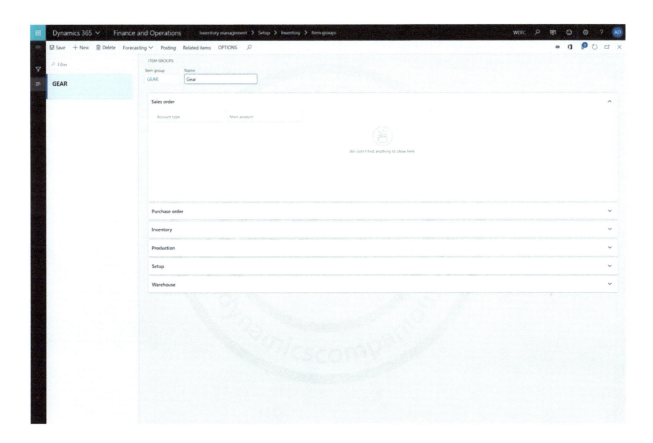

Step 3: Update the Name

And then we can add a more descriptive name for the item group.

To do this just update the **Name** value.

This time, we will want to set the **Name** to **Gear**.

dync
www.dynamicscompanions.com
Dynamics Companions

- 107 -

www.blindsquirrelpublishing.com
© 2019 Blind Squirrel Publishing, LLC , All Rights Reserved

BLIND SQUIRREL
PUBLISHING

Adding a new Item Group

How to do it...

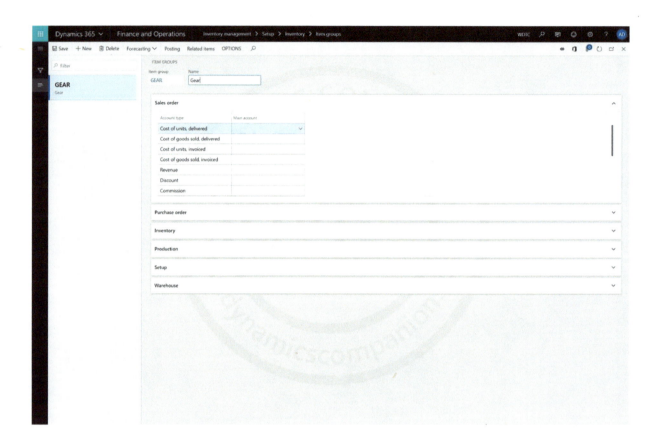

Step 4: Click on the Save button

After we have done that we can save the record.

To do this just click on the **Save** button.

Notice that when we saved the record, a number of new items showed up in the body of the form for the default accounts to use for different posting actions.

We will return to these later on when we start buying, selling, and inventorying our products.

Review

Congratulations. We have set up the item groups which we will need when we set up the products in the next step.

dync
dynamics companions
www.dynamicscompanions.com
Dynamics Companions

- 109 -

www.blindsquirrelpublishing.com
© 2019 Blind Squirrel Publishing, LLC , All Rights Reserved

BLIND SQUIRREL
PUBLISHING

Adding a New Product

Now that we have the minimum set of control codes configured for the products, we can move on and set up a product in the system.

Topics Covered

- Opening the Released Product Maintenance workspace

- Creating a new Released Product

- Adding an Image to the Product

- Assigning the Product an Item Model Group

- Updating the Product Dimension Groups

- Assigning the Product an Item Group

- Validating the Product

Opening the Released Product Maintenance workspace

To do this we will want to find the **Release product** maintenance workspace.

How to do it...

Step 1: Open the Released product maintenance form through the menu search

We can find the **Released product** maintenance workspace through the menu search feature.

Type in released prod m into the menu search and select Released product maintenance.

dync
dynamics companion

www.dynamicscompanions.com
Dynamics Companions

- 111 -

www.blindsquirrelpublishing.com
© 2019 Blind Squirrel Publishing, LLC , All Rights Reserved

BLIND SQUIRREL
PUBLISHING

Opening the Released Product Maintenance workspace

How to do it...

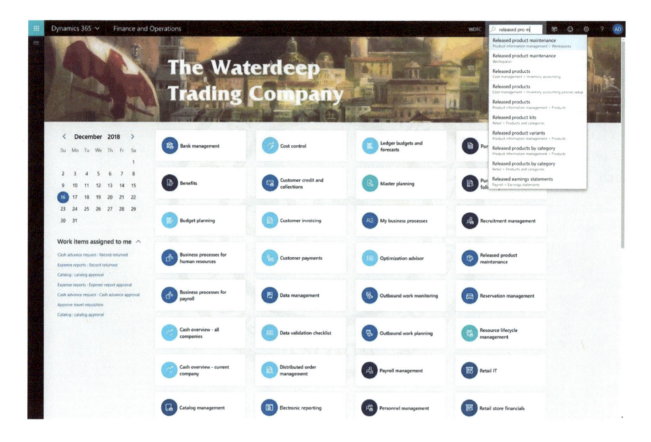

Step 1: Open the Released product maintenance form through the menu search

We can find the **Released product** maintenance workspace through the menu search feature.

We can do this by clicking on the search icon in the header of the form (or by pressing **ALT+G**) and then type in **released prod m** into the search box. Then you will be able to select the **Released product maintenance** workspace from the dropdown list.

www.dynamicscompanions.com
Dynamics Companions

- 112 -

www.blindsquirrelpublishing.com
© 2019 Blind Squirrel Publishing, LLC , All Rights Reserved

BLIND SQUIRREL
PUBLISHING

Opening the Released Product Maintenance workspace

How to do it...

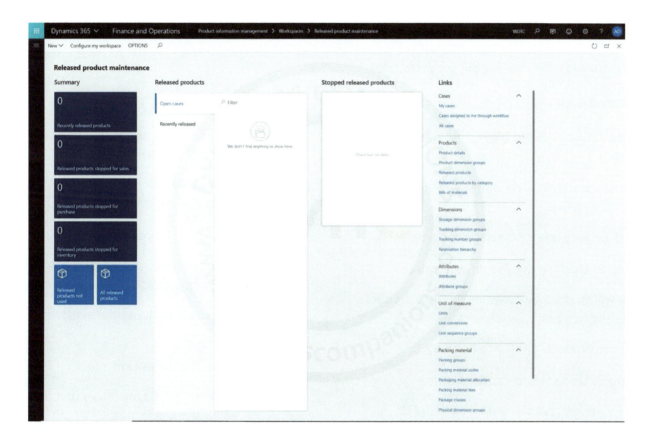

Step 1: Open the Released product maintenance form through the menu search

This will open up the **Released product maintenance** workspace which will allow us to see a lot of information about all of our product in one place.

dync
dynamics companions

www.dynamicscompanions.com
Dynamics Companions

- 113 -

www.blindsquirrelpublishing.com
© 2019 Blind Squirrel Publishing, LLC, All Rights Reserved

BLIND SQUIRREL
PUBLISHING

Creating a new Released Product

Now we can start creating our products.

How to do it...

Step 1: Click on the New + Released product button

We will start off by creating a new Released product record.

Click on the New + Released product button.

Step 2: Update the Product number

We will start off by assigning our new product a product number.

Set the Product number to BACKPACK.

Step 3: Update the Product name

Then we will give our product a name to accompany the product number.

Set the Product name to Backpack.

Step 4: Select the Inventory unit

We will now want to specify the different units of measure that we will be using for this product.

We will start off by selecting the unit that we will be tracking the inventory in.

Click on the **Inventory unit** dropdown list And choose **ea**.

Step 5: Choose the Purchase unit

Next, we will select the unit of measure that we will be purchasing the product in.

Click on the **Purchase unit** dropdown list And select **ea**.

Step 6: Choose the Sales unit

And then we will select the inventory unit that we will be selling the product in.

Click on the **Sales unit** dropdown list And choose **ea**.

Step 7: Click on the OK button

After we have done that we can create the product record.

Click on the **OK** button.

Creating a new Released Product

How to do it...

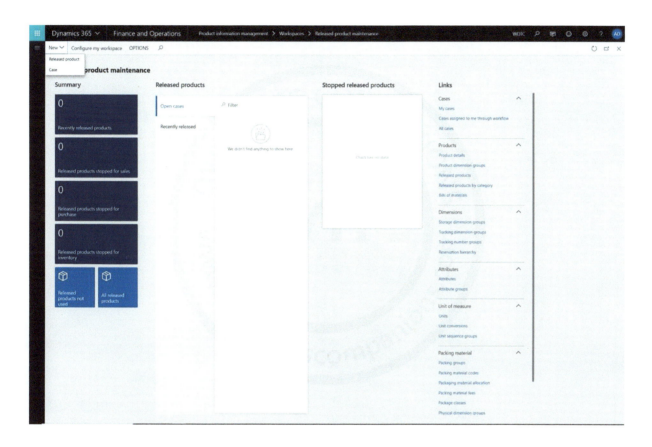

Step 1: Click on the New + Released product button

We will start off by creating a new Released product record.

To do this, all we need to do is click on the **New + Released product** button.

www.dynamicscompanions.com
Dynamics Companions

- 115 -

www.blindsquirrelpublishing.com
© 2019 Blind Squirrel Publishing, LLC, All Rights Reserved

BLIND SQUIRREL
PUBLISHING

Creating a new Released Product

How to do it...

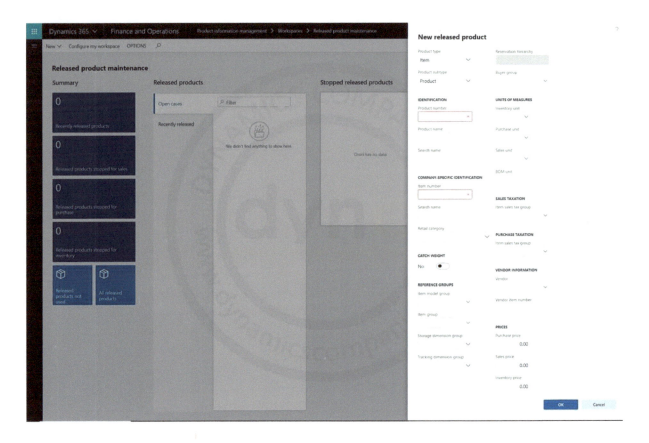

Step 1: Click on the New + Released product button

This will open up the **New released product** quick setup panel.

dync
dynamics companions
www.dynamicscompanions.com
Dynamics Companions

- 116 -

www.blindsquirrelpublishing.com
© 2019 Blind Squirrel Publishing, LLC , All Rights Reserved

BLIND SQUIRREL
PUBLISHING

Creating a new Released Product

How to do it...

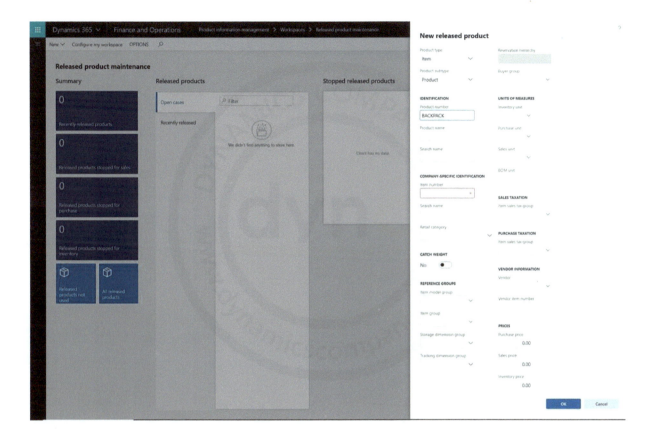

Step 2: Update the Product number

We will start off by assigning our new product a product number.

To do this, we will just need to change the **Product number** value.

For this example, we will want to set the **Product number** to **BACKPACK**.

dync
dynamics companions
www.dynamicscompanions.com
Dynamics Companions
- 117 -
www.blindsquirrelpublishing.com
© 2019 Blind Squirrel Publishing, LLC, All Rights Reserved
BLIND SQUIRREL
PUBLISHING

Creating a new Released Product

How to do it...

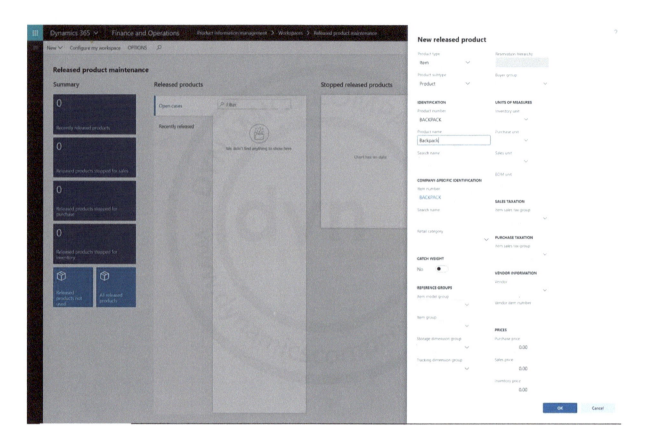

Step 3: Update the Product name

Then we will give our product a name to accompany the product number.

To do this just change the **Product name** value.

For this example, we will want to set the **Product name** to **Backpack**.

dync
dynamics companions

www.dynamicscompanions.com
Dynamics Companions

- 118 -

www.blindsquirrelpublishing.com
© 2019 Blind Squirrel Publishing, LLC , All Rights Reserved

BLIND SQUIRREL
PUBLISHING

Creating a new Released Product

How to do it...

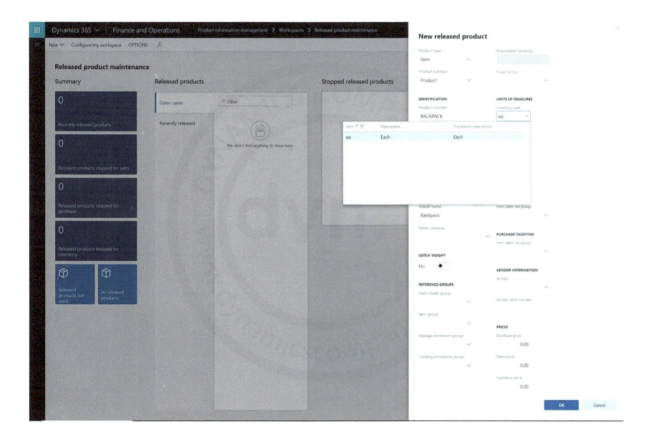

Step 4: Select the Inventory unit

We will now want to specify the different units of measure that we will be using for this product.

We will start off by selecting the unit that we will be tracking the inventory in.

To do this just pick the **Inventory unit** value from the dropdown list.

This time, we will want to click on the **Inventory unit** dropdown list and select **ea**.

dync
dynamics companions

www.dynamicscompanions.com
Dynamics Companions

- 119 -

www.blindsquirrelpublishing.com
© 2019 Blind Squirrel Publishing, LLC , All Rights Reserved

BLIND SQUIRREL
PUBLISHING

Creating a new Released Product

How to do it...

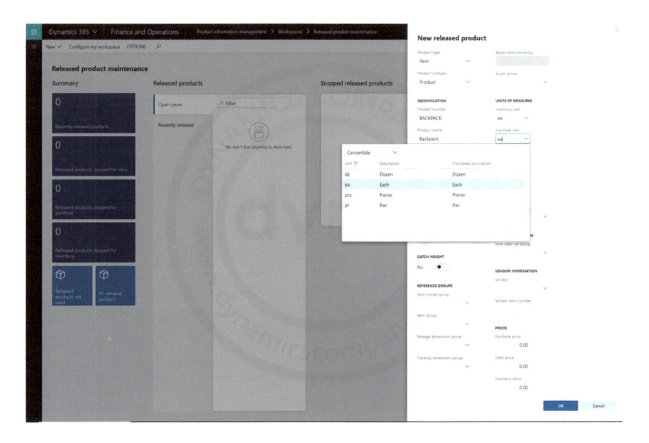

Step 5: Choose the Purchase unit

Next, we will select the unit of measure that we will be purchasing the product in.

To do this, we will just need to select the **Purchase unit** option from the dropdown list.

For this example, we will want to click on the **Purchase unit** dropdown list and pick **ea**.

dync
dynamics companions

www.dynamicscompanions.com
Dynamics Companions

- 120 -

www.blindsquirrelpublishing.com
© 2019 Blind Squirrel Publishing, LLC , All Rights Reserved

BLIND SQUIRREL
PUBLISHING

Creating a new Released Product

How to do it...

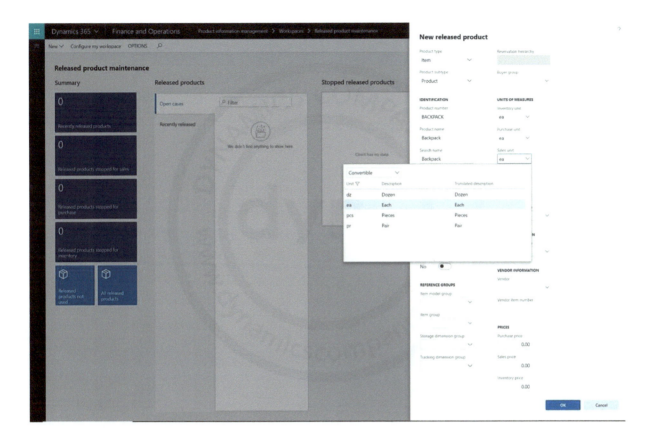

Step 6: Choose the Sales unit

And then we will select the inventory unit that we will be selling the product in.

To do this, we will just need to select the **Sales unit** option from the dropdown list.

For this example, we will want to click on the **Sales unit** dropdown list and pick **ea**.

dync
dynamics companions

www.dynamicscompanions.com
Dynamics Companions

- 121 -

www.blindsquirrelpublishing.com
© 2019 Blind Squirrel Publishing, LLC , All Rights Reserved

BLIND SQUIRREL
PUBLISHING

Creating a new Released Product

How to do it...

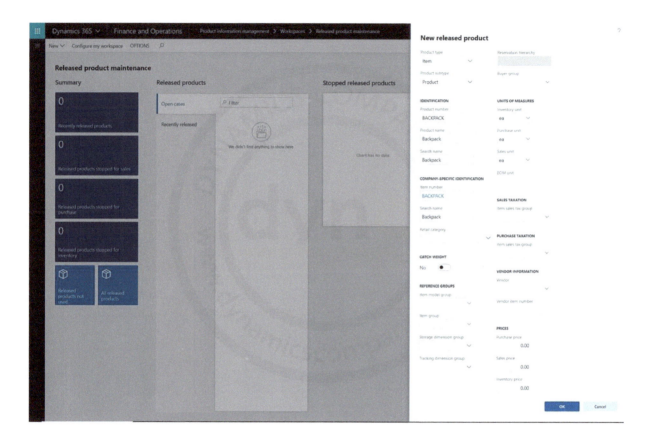

Step 7: Click on the OK button

After we have done that we can create the product record.

To do this, all we need to do is click on the **OK** button.

www.dynamicscompanions.com
Dynamics Companions

- 122 -

www.blindsquirrelpublishing.com
© 2019 Blind Squirrel Publishing, LLC , All Rights Reserved

BLIND SQUIRREL
PUBLISHING

Creating a new Released Product

How to do it...

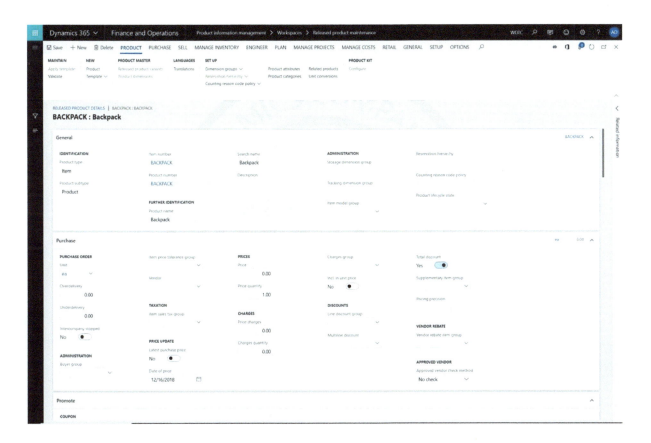

Step 7: Click on the OK button

That will then create the product for us, and we will be taken to the full view of the product with all of the information that we can configure against the Released product.

dync
www.dynamicscompanions.com
Dynamics Companions

- 123 -

www.blindsquirrelpublishing.com
© 2019 Blind Squirrel Publishing, LLC , All Rights Reserved

BLIND SQUIRREL
PUBLISHING

Adding an Image to the Product

If we want, we can add an image to the product to accompany it within the system.

How to do it...

Step 1: Click on the Related information button

To do this, we will want to expand out the **Related information** tab.

Click on the **Related information** button.

Step 2: Click on the Change image button

This will open up the **Related information** panel where we will see that there are some additional fact boxes that are associated with the released product.

We are interested in the one that has the **Product image** information, and right now it is blank, so we will want to change the image for the product.

Click on the **Change image** button.

Step 3: Click on the New button

This will open up the **Product images** dialog box where we will be able to add a new image.

Click on the **New** button.

Step 4: Click on the Browse button

When the **Upload documents** panel is shown, we will be able to upload a new image.

Click on the **Browse** button.

Step 5: Click on the Open button

This will open up the file explorer, and we can select the backpack image from our product gallery.

Click on the **Open** button.

Step 6: Click on the OK button

After we have done that we will see the image within the product gallery and we can continue on.

Click on the **OK** button.

Adding an Image to the Product

How to do it...

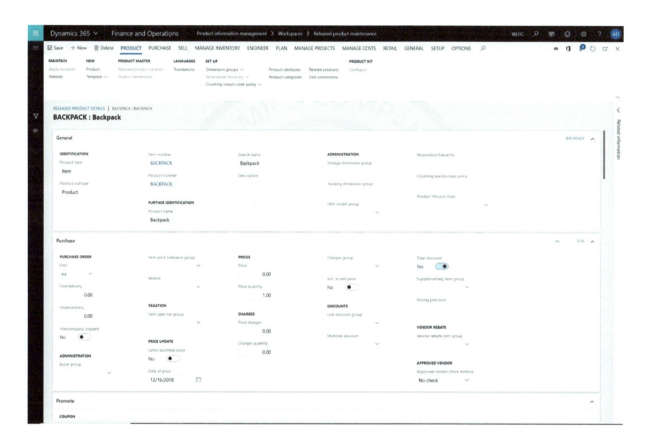

Step 1: Click on the Related information button

To do this, we will want to expand out the **Related information** tab.

To do this, all we need to do is click on the **Related information** button.

Adding an Image to the Product

How to do it...

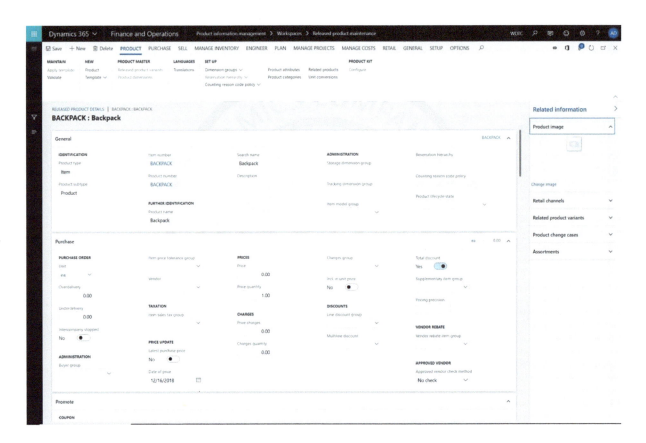

Step 2: Click on the Change image button

This will open up the **Related information** panel where we will see that there are some additional fact boxes that are associated with the released product.

We are interested in the one that has the **Product image** information, and right now it is blank, so we will want to change the image for the product.

To do this just click on the **Change image** button.

www.dynamicscompanions.com
Dynamics Companions

- 126 -

www.blindsquirrelpublishing.com
© 2019 Blind Squirrel Publishing, LLC , All Rights Reserved

BLIND SQUIRREL
PUBLISHING

Adding an Image to the Product

How to do it...

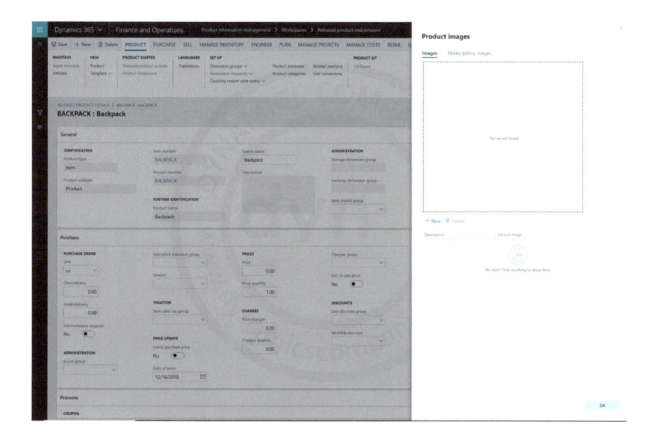

Step 3: Click on the New button

This will open up the **Product images** dialog box where we will be able to add a new image.

To do this, all we need to do is click on the **New** button.

dync
www.dynamicscompanions.com
Dynamics Companions
- 127 -
www.blindsquirrelpublishing.com
© 2019 Blind Squirrel Publishing, LLC , All Rights Reserved
BLIND SQUIRREL
PUBLISHING

Adding an Image to the Product

How to do it...

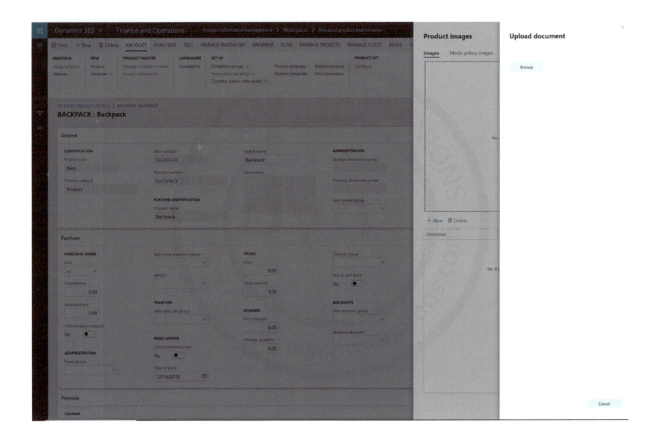

Step 4: Click on the Browse button

When the **Upload documents** panel is shown, we will be able to upload a new image.

To do this just click on the **Browse** button.

dync
dynamics companions
www.dynamicscompanions.com
Dynamics Companions

- 128 -

www.blindsquirrelpublishing.com
© 2019 Blind Squirrel Publishing, LLC , All Rights Reserved

BLIND SQUIRREL
PUBLISHING

Adding an Image to the Product

How to do it...

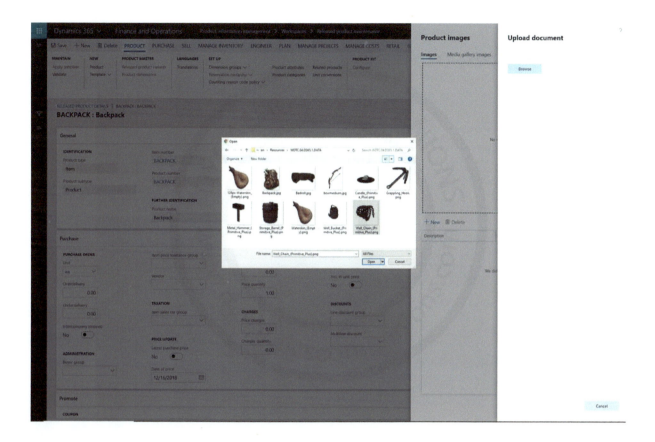

Step 5: Click on the Open button

This will open up the file explorer, and we can select the backpack image from our product gallery.

To do this, all we need to do is click on the **Open** button.

www.dynamicscompanions.com
Dynamics Companions

- 129 -

www.blindsquirrelpublishing.com
© 2019 Blind Squirrel Publishing, LLC , All Rights Reserved

BLIND SQUIRREL
PUBLISHING

Adding an Image to the Product

How to do it...

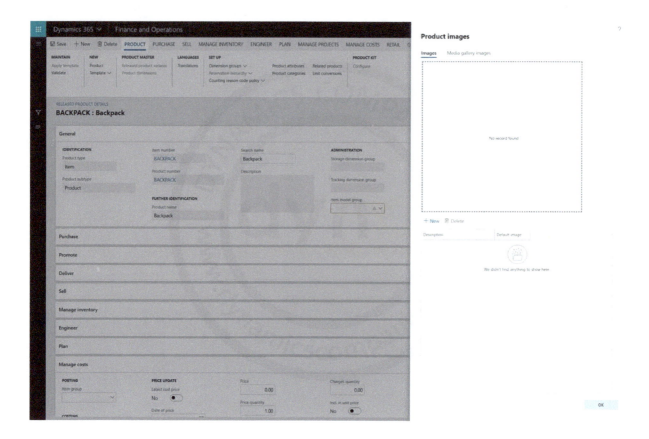

Step 6: Click on the OK button

After we have done that we will see the image within the product gallery and we can continue on.

To do this just click on the **OK** button.

www.dynamicscompanions.com
Dynamics Companions

- 130 -

www.blindsquirrelpublishing.com
© 2019 Blind Squirrel Publishing, LLC , All Rights Reserved

BLIND SQUIRREL
PUBLISHING

Adding an Image to the Product

How to do it...

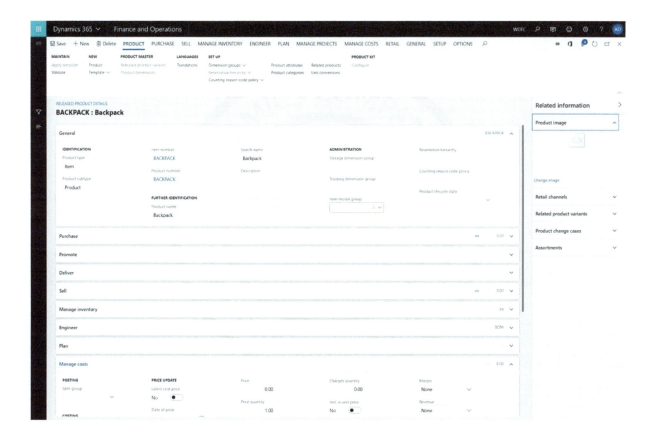

Step 6: Click on the OK button

When we return back to the **Released product** page, we will then see the image in the **Related information** panel.

dync
dynamics companions
www.dynamicscompanions.com
Dynamics Companions

- 131 -

www.blindsquirrelpublishing.com
© 2019 Blind Squirrel Publishing, LLC , All Rights Reserved

BLIND SQUIRREL
PUBLISHING

Assigning the Product an Item Model Group

Next we will want to tweak the settings of the product, and we will start off by associating the product with an Item model group.

How to do it...

Step 1: Select the Item model group

We will be able to do this by selecting the item model group that we just set up.

Click on the **Item model group** dropdown list
And choose **GEAR**.

Assigning the Product an Item Model Group

How to do it...

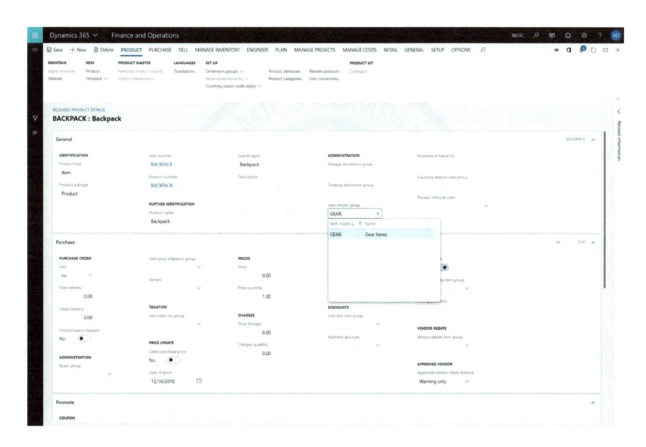

Step 1: Select the Item model group

We will be able to do this by selecting the item model group that we just set up.

To do this just select the **Item model group** option from the dropdown list.

This time, we will want to click on the **Item model group** dropdown list and select **GEAR**.

dync
dynamics companions

www.dynamicscompanions.com
Dynamics Companions

- 133 -

www.blindsquirrelpublishing.com
© 2019 Blind Squirrel Publishing, LLC , All Rights Reserved

BLIND SQUIRREL
PUBLISHING

Updating the Product Dimension Groups

Next we will want to configure the dimension groups for the product.

How to do it...

Step 1: Click on the Dimension groups button

We can find the dimension groups within the Products action bar.

Click on the **Dimension groups** button.

Step 2: Select the Storage dimension group

We will start off by selecting the way that we will be storing the product in the warehouse.

Click on the **Storage dimension group** dropdown list And choose **SiteWHLoc**.

Step 3: Choose the Tracking dimension group

And then we will want to select the way that we will want to track the inventory.

Click on the **Tracking dimension group** dropdown list And choose **None**.

Step 4: Click on the OK button

After we have done that we can save the changes.

Click on the **OK** button.

Updating the Product Dimension Groups

How to do it...

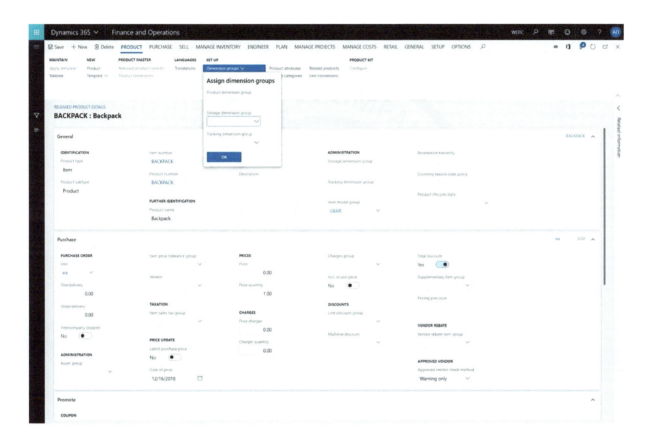

Step 1: Click on the Dimension groups button

We can find the dimension groups within the Products action bar.

To do this, all we need to do is click on the **Dimension groups** button.

www.dynamicscompanions.com
Dynamics Companions

- 135 -

www.blindsquirrelpublishing.com
© 2019 Blind Squirrel Publishing, LLC , All Rights Reserved

BLIND SQUIRREL
PUBLISHING

Updating the Product Dimension Groups

How to do it...

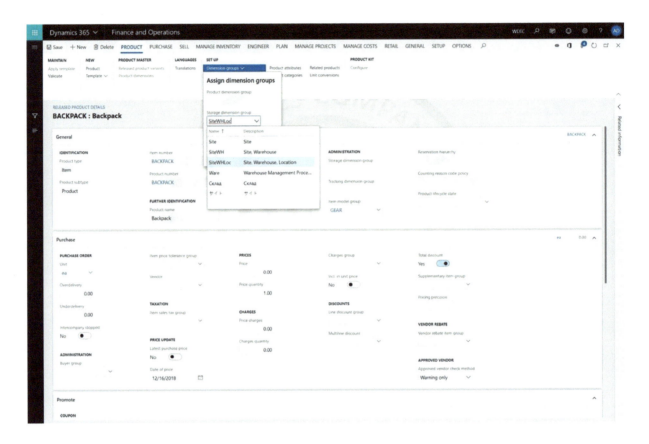

Step 2: Select the Storage dimension group

We will start off by selecting the way that we will be storing the product in the warehouse.

To do this just pick the **Storage dimension group** option from the dropdown list.

This time, we will want to click on the **Storage dimension group** dropdown list and select **SiteWHLoc**.

dync
dynamics companions
www.dynamicscompanions.com
Dynamics Companions

- 136 -

www.blindsquirrelpublishing.com
© 2019 Blind Squirrel Publishing, LLC , All Rights Reserved

BLIND SQUIRREL
PUBLISHING

Updating the Product Dimension Groups

How to do it...

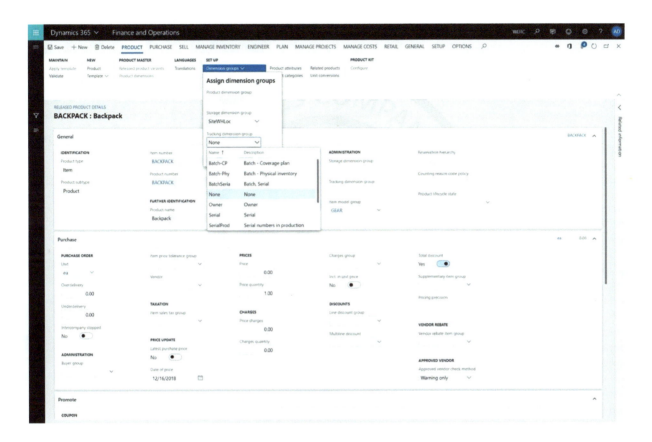

Step 3: Choose the Tracking dimension group

And then we will want to select the way that we will want to track the inventory.

To do this, we will just need to select the **Tracking dimension group** option from the dropdown list.

This time, we will want to click on the **Tracking dimension group** dropdown list and pick **None**.

dync
dynamics companions

www.dynamicscompanions.com
Dynamics Companions

- 137 -

www.blindsquirrelpublishing.com
© 2019 Blind Squirrel Publishing, LLC, All Rights Reserved

BLIND SQUIRREL
PUBLISHING

Updating the Product Dimension Groups

How to do it...

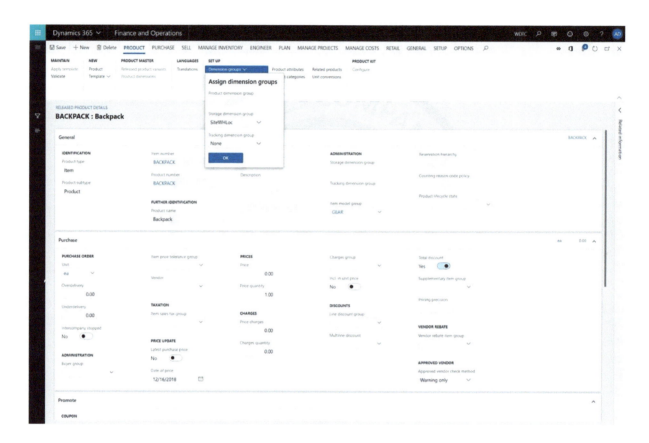

Step 4: Click on the OK button

After we have done that we can save the changes.

To do this just click on the **OK** button.

dync
www.dynamicscompanions.com
Dynamics Companions

- 138 -

www.blindsquirrelpublishing.com
© 2019 Blind Squirrel Publishing, LLC , All Rights Reserved

BLIND SQUIRREL
PUBLISHING

Updating the Product Dimension Groups

How to do it...

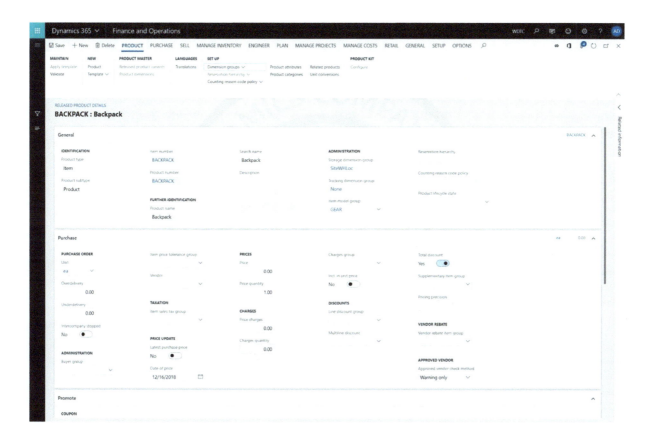

Step 4: Click on the OK button

Now we will see that the **Storage dimension group** and the **Tracking dimension group** has been updated on the product.

dync
www.dynamicscompanions.com
Dynamics Companions

- 139 -

www.blindsquirrelpublishing.com
© 2019 Blind Squirrel Publishing, LLC , All Rights Reserved

BLIND SQUIRREL
PUBLISHING

Assigning the Product an Item Group

Next we will want to assign our product to an Item group so that the system will know how to post to the ledger.

How to do it...

Step 1: Click on the Collapse all button

The item group is further down in one of the fast tabs. To quickly see all of the different configuration tabs we will collapse them all.

Right-mouse-click on the tab heading and then select the **Collapse all** button.

Step 2: Click on the Manage costs tab

Click on the **Manage costs** tabs.

Step 3: Select the Item group

Now we can select the Item group that we want to associate with the product.

Click on the **Item group** dropdown list And select **GEAR**.

Assigning the Product an Item Group

How to do it...

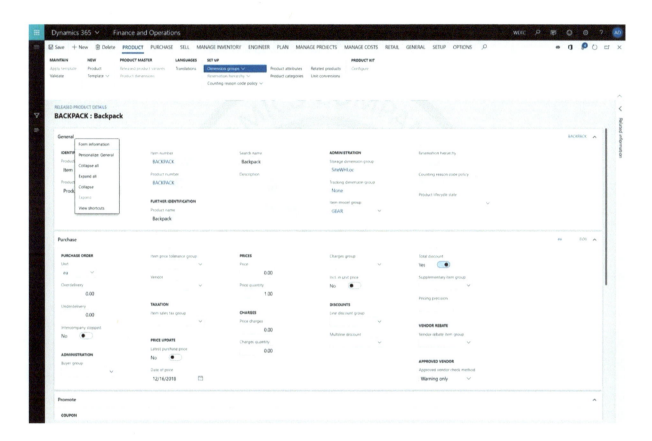

Step 1: Click on the Collapse all button

The item group is further down in one of the fast tabs. To quickly see all of the different configuration tabs we will collapse them all.

To do this all we need to do is right-mouse-click on the tab heading and then select the **Collapse all** button.

dync
dynamics companions

www.dynamicscompanions.com
Dynamics Companions

- 141 -

www.blindsquirrelpublishing.com
© 2019 Blind Squirrel Publishing, LLC , All Rights Reserved

BLIND SQUIRREL
PUBLISHING

Assigning the Product an Item Group

How to do it...

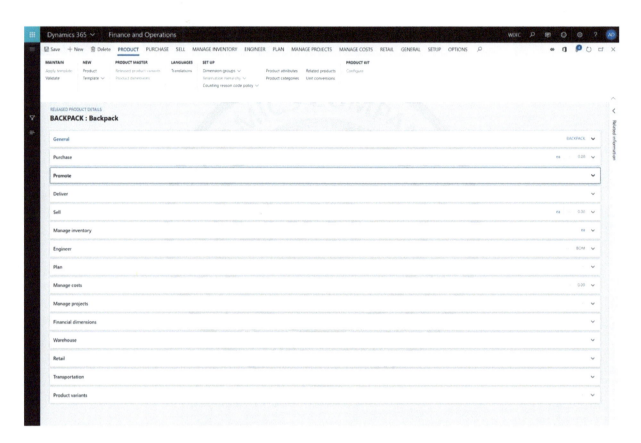

Step 1: Click on the Collapse all button

This will allow us to see all of the Fast Tabs.

dync
dynamics companions

www.dynamicscompanions.com
Dynamics Companions

- 142 -

www.blindsquirrelpublishing.com
© 2019 Blind Squirrel Publishing, LLC , All Rights Reserved

BLIND SQUIRREL
PUBLISHING

Assigning the Product an Item Group

How to do it...

Step 2: Click on the Manage costs tab

To do this, all we need to do is click on the **Manage costs** tab.

dync
dynamics companions
www.dynamicscompanions.com
Dynamics Companions

- 143 -

www.blindsquirrelpublishing.com
© 2019 Blind Squirrel Publishing, LLC , All Rights Reserved

BLIND SQUIRREL
PUBLISHING

Assigning the Product an Item Group

How to do it...

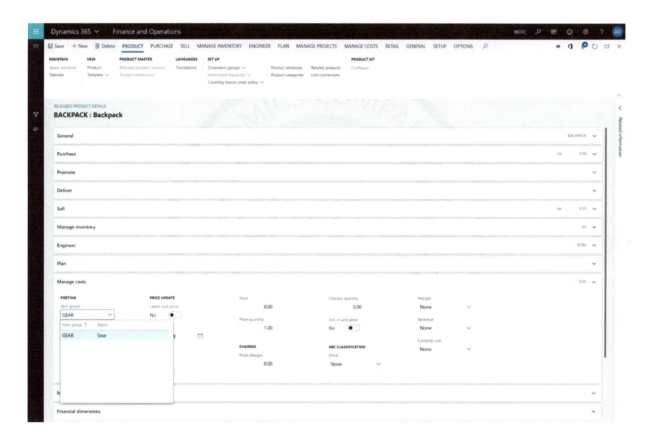

Step 3: Select the Item group

Now we can select the Item group that we want to associate with the product.

To do this, we will just need to select the **Item group** value from the dropdown list.

For this example, we will want to click on the **Item group** dropdown list and pick **GEAR**.

dync
dynamics companions
www.dynamicscompanions.com
Dynamics Companions

- 144 -

www.blindsquirrelpublishing.com
© 2019 Blind Squirrel Publishing, LLC , All Rights Reserved

BLIND SQUIRREL
PUBLISHING

Validating the Product

After we have done that, we can make sure that everything is set up correctly on the **Released product** details by validating the product.

How to do it...

Step 1: Click on the Validate button

To do this, we just kick off the validation process.

Click on the **Validate** button.

Validating the Product

How to do it...

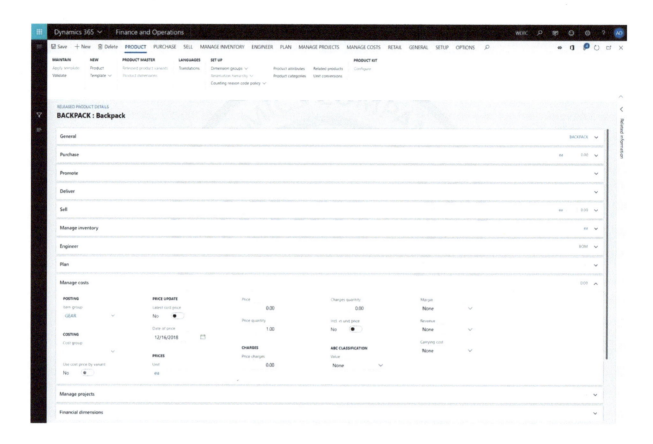

Step 1: Click on the Validate button

To do this, we just kick off the validation process.

To do this, all we need to do is click on the **Validate** button.

www.dynamicscompanions.com
Dynamics Companions

- 146 -

www.blindsquirrelpublishing.com
© 2019 Blind Squirrel Publishing, LLC , All Rights Reserved

BLIND SQUIRREL
PUBLISHING

Validating the Product

How to do it...

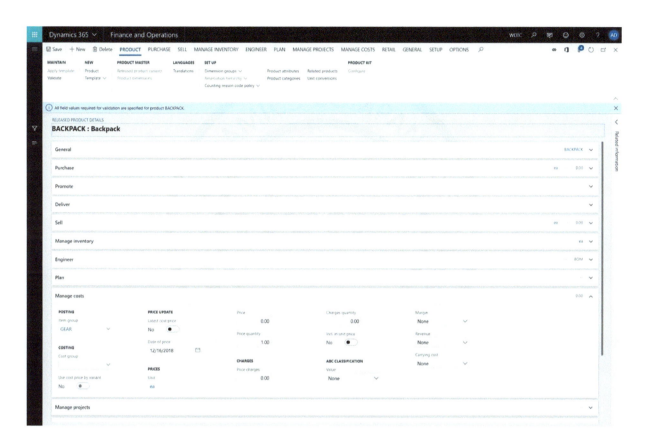

Step 1: Click on the Validate button

If everything is set up correctly, we will see a message that tells us that the product is set up and ready to use.

www.dynamicscompanions.com
Dynamics Companions

- 147 -

www.blindsquirrelpublishing.com
© 2019 Blind Squirrel Publishing, LLC , All Rights Reserved

BLIND SQUIRREL
PUBLISHING

Review

Congratulations. You now have your first product in the system that you can start using.

Summary

Great work. Now we have a released product configured, and we have also set up the codes and controls for how the product is tracked in inventory, and also the starting configuration for the default posting codes for the product as well.

dyn c
dynamics companions

www.dynamicscompanions.com
Dynamics Companions

- 149 -

www.blindsquirrelpublishing.com
© 2019 Blind Squirrel Publishing, LLC , All Rights Reserved

BLIND SQUIRREL
PUBLISHING

Conclusion

How easy was that? We just created our warehouse with inventory locations, and then created the first product that we will be able to use within the warehouse.

We are rocking and rolling now.

About The Author

Murray Fife is an Author of over 25 books on Microsoft Dynamics including the Bare Bones Configuration Guide series of over 15 books which step the user through the setup of initial Dynamics instance, then through the Financial modules and then through the configuration of the more specialized modules like production, service management, and project accounting. You can find all his books on Amazon at **www.amazon.com/author/murrayfife**.

For more information on Murray, here is his contact information:

If you are interested in contacting Murray or want to follow his blogs and posts then here is all of his contact information:

Email: murray@murrayfife.com

Twitter: @murrayfife

Facebook: faceook.com/murraycfife

Google: google.com/+murrayfife

LinkedIn: linkedin.com/in/murrayfife

Blog: atinkerersnotebook.com

SlideShare: slideshare.net/murrayfife

Amazon: amazon.com/author/murrayfife

dync
www.dynamicscompanions.com
Dynamics Companions
- 151 -
www.blindsquirrelpublishing.com
© 2019 Blind Squirrel Publishing, LLC , All Rights Reserved
BLIND SQUIRREL
PUBLISHING

www.ingramcontent.com/pod-product-compliance
Lightning Source LLC
Chambersburg PA
CBHW041417050326

40689CB00002B/551